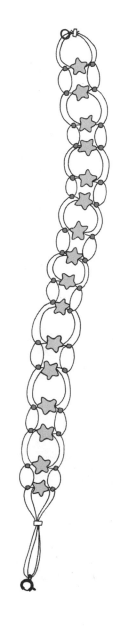

Jazzy Jewelry

Power Beads, Crystals, Chokers, & Illusion and Tattoo Styles

Diane Baker

Illustrations by Alexandra Michaels

WILLIAMSON PUBLISHING • CHARLOTTE, VERMONT

Library of Congress Cataloging-in-Publication Data

Baker, Diane.
    Jazzy jewelry : power beads, crystals, chokers, and illusion and tattoo styles / Diane Baker.
        p. cm. — (A Williamson kids can! book)
    ISBN 1-885593-47-3 (pbk.)
    1. Beadwork—Juvenile literature. 2. Jewelry making—Juvenile literature. [1. Beadwork.
    2. Jewelry making. 3. Handicraft.] I. Title. II. Series.

    TT860 .B32 2000
    745.594'2—dc21

                                                    00-043712

Kids Can!® series editor: **Susan Williamson**
Project editor: **Vicky Congdon**
Illustrations: **Alexandra Michaels**
Interior design and back cover : **Linda Williamson, Dawson Design**
Front cover design: **Alexandra Michaels**
Cover photo: **Rose McNulty**
Printing: **Capital City Press**

Williamson Publishing Co.
P. O. Box 185
Charlotte, VT 05445
(800) 234-8791

Manufactured in the United States of America

10 9 8 7 6 5 4 3 2 1

Little Hands®, *Kids Can!*®, *Tales Alive!*®, and *Kaleidoscope Kids*® are registered trademarks of Williamson Publishing.

Good Times™ and *Quick Starts for Kids!*™ are trademarks of Williamson Publishing.

DEDICATION

To my dear parents, Ben and Phyllis Adler, who supported my hobbies with patience, enthusiasm, and supplies; to my daughters, Vivian and Brigit, may their creative spirits always thrive; and to Todd, whose love and care are part of every enterprise of our home.

This book is for all the girls who love making things, and for the work of their heads, hands, and hearts.

ACKNOWLEDGMENTS

Thank you to my wise and generous advisors: Lisa Claxton, beader *extraordinaire* from Baubles and Beads in Berkeley, California, for answering many questions and sharing ideas; and Emily Marks, a true friend and co-crafter. I'm grateful to my amazing neighborhood friends for a billion favors. Your support and companionship brought that peace of mind and connectedness that nourishes creativity. Thanks also to the cabin crew for so much good company and cooking.

My daughters and their friends supplied great feedback and suggestions for each project. Natalie and Sarah Rosen were special helpers.

I'm grateful to Vicky Congdon, my editor at Williamson, an encouraging and expert editor, and, as a terrific bonus, cheerful and fun.

Like most great projects, this book is a product of teamwork.

My deepest thanks go to Alexandra Michaels, who did amazing work illustrating this book. With style, clarity, an incredible amount of caring labor, and her own special jazz, she guides crafters through the steps of creating all the jewelry here.

And more thanks to Linda Williamson, the designer who combined the voices of my writing and Alex's art with her know-how and vision and made them sing in harmony!

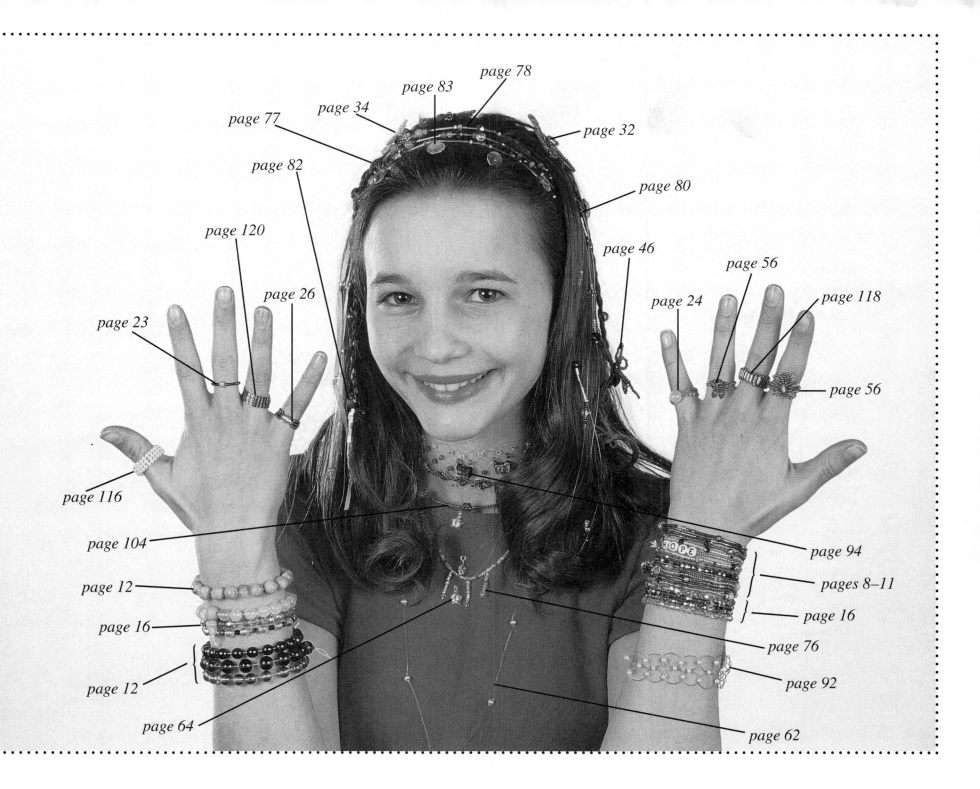

page 78

page 83

page 34

page 77

page 32

page 82

page 80

page 120

page 46

page 56

page 26

page 24

page 118

page 23

page 56

page 116

page 104

page 94

page 12

pages 8–11

page 16

page 16

page 76

page 12

page 92

page 64

page 62

CONTENTS

Why Make Your Own Jewelry?

We see great jewelry in shops all the time. Much of it is good-looking and inexpensive. So why should you bother making your own?

The #1 Reason: It's Fun!

Making jewelry can be as relaxing or as challenging as you want. With so many designs and styles to create and a world full of beautiful beads to collect, how could you ever be bored again?

It Makes You Smarter!

It's true! While you're making all these beautiful things to wear, you're exercising a big chunk of your mind! It takes brain power to visualize a piece of jewelry in your mind and then make it into something solid and real. You're taking an idea from the "thinking about it" stage to the "creating it and finishing it" stage (a very handy skill).

It's Better (and Cheaper)

The reason jewelry in stores is sometimes inexpensive is because the manufacturers aren't using high-quality materials or crafting. They use plastic beads instead of glass, for example. Or, they may offer only one or two currently popular colors. Making your own usually means spending less and ending up with a better-quality piece.

You Can Have It *Your* Way

When you make your own jewelry, you can have exactly what you like: the exact style, the exact color, the exact length. You can recreate what you've admired in the store (or on a friend!), or you can experiment with your own ideas (hey, you just might start a hot new style!).

You'll Get Better Acquainted with an Awesome Person – You!

When you create something yourself, you'll make decisions large (Which bracelet style in this chapter goes best with this necklace?) and small (Which accent bead looks best at the end of this strand?). Each one teaches you a little more about what you like and dislike.

So, ready to get started?

If you've done any beading or craft projects at home before, you may already have what you need to jump right into some of the easier designs.

You'll find a list of the basic beading supplies and handy tools needed for all the jewelry in this book on pages 124–138.

Power Beads, Austrian Crystals, and Other Simple Strands

A single strand full of beads — bracelet, necklace, anklet, or ring — is the simplest bead jewelry. Strands are so easy to make, you won't believe you've been buying them! In the time it takes you to find one you like enough to buy, you can make your own in your favorite colors, length, and bead styles.

Wear just one — or load yourself up!

The "As-Simple-As-It-Gets" Bead Bracelet

Make one — or make a dozen! — for your wrists or ankles. With a bit more thread and a few more beads, it's a necklace!

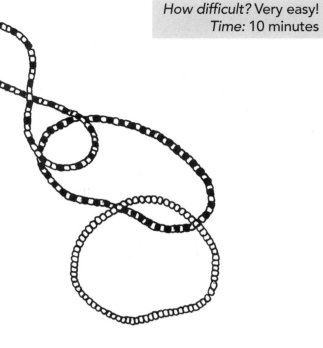

1 Secure one end of the thread with a piece of tape; thread the other end through the needle. String enough beads to go around your wrist.

2 Tie the ends with a lock knot*. Trim the threads.

WHAT YOU NEED
10" (25 cm) of elastic thread
Tape
Beading needle
Seed beads (about 110), in the color(s) of your choice
Scissors

*See Techniques, pages 124–130.

Oh, So Charming!

Add charms, accent beads, or the very latest style — sequins! — to the strands as you string, or hang them from a jump ring* so they dangle. It's very quick and easy to make a wristful of different bracelets — then, pile them on!

Multitudes of "Multistrands."

Wearing multiple strands of bracelets looks especially jazzy when they all pass through a large accent bead, like a crystal, a pearl, or a colorful ceramic bead. Just follow these steps!

It's a Wrap!

Here's another popular look: Join three or four bracelets by wrapping a 4" (10 cm) strand around them as shown and knotting the ends in a lock knot*.

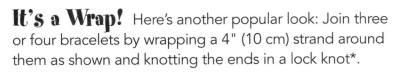

SEASONAL SENSATIONS

Celebrate the holidays with these special bracelets and necklaces — ready in minutes! Seed bead strands are so quick and easy to make, you can do a special event bracelet, then cut it up and use the beads for an all-new look!

- **For the Fourth of July:** *Wrap red, white, and blue strands together (see It's a Wrap!, page 9).*
- **For Christmas:** *Wrap strands of red, green, and white.*
- **For Chanukah:** *Hold a blue strand and a white strand together and knot them with a double knot* as shown.*

  And how about a red-and-yellow version for the winter solstice to celebrate the return of the sun?

  For a necklace, space the knots 2" (5 cm) apart.

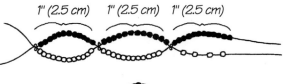

1" (2.5 cm) 1" (2.5 cm) 1" (2.5 cm)

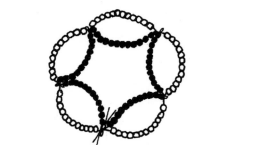

The Inside Scoop
Stringing Beads

Although you want to string the beads snugly against each other (so the thread won't show), be careful to allow enough stretch so you can slip the piece of jewelry on comfortably. Leave 2" to 3" (5 to 7.5 cm) of unstrung elastic at the end so you can tie a knot easily, too.

*See Techniques, pages 124–130.

Elemental Seed Bead Bracelets

You can wear these four bracelets individually or as a set.

1 Cut a piece of thread approximately 10" (25 cm) long. Secure one end of the thread with a piece of tape; thread the other end through the needle. String one color of seed beads. When you think your bracelet is almost long enough, try it around your wrist.

2 Add the alphabet beads to spell the element that color represents.

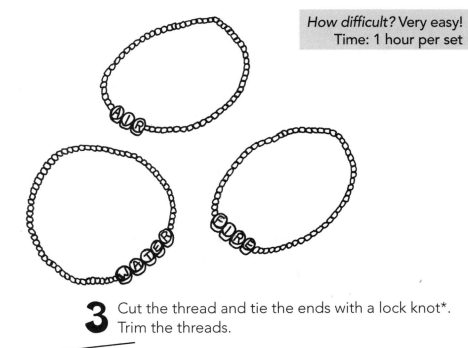

How difficult? Very easy!
Time: 1 hour per set

3 Cut the thread and tie the ends with a lock knot*. Trim the threads.

4 Repeat for each of the three other colors. Wear as many strands together as you like.

WHAT YOU NEED
Scissors
40" (100 cm) of elastic thread
Tape
Beading needle
4 tubes of seed beads in green, white, red, and blue
Alphabet beads to spell "EARTH," "AIR," "FIRE," "WATER"

THE ELEMENTS

Some cultures refer to the earth, air, fire, and water as elements that have sacred meaning. They match these elements to human qualities and symbolize them with color.

EARTH *(green): body, health*   AIR *(white): thought, humor*
FIRE *(red): spirit, courage*   WATER *(blue): feelings and emotions*

See Techniques, pages 124–130.

Power Bead Bracelet

*The very popular power bead bracelets are simple strands of beads made of semiprecious stones or glass. They're usually tied off with special "T" and cap beads that pull the elastic thread up and into view. Quick, easy, and inexpensive to make, power bead bracelets in a mix of colors are **the** look!*

To make the bracelet:

Secure one end of the thread with a piece of tape; thread the other end through the needle. String as many beads as you need to go around your wrist.

To finish with a "T" bead:

1 Twist the short piece of beading wire to form a small loop at one end.

Insert the loop into the top hole of the "T" bead.

Pull the needle and thread through the side holes *and* the loop.

Unthread the elastic from the needle.

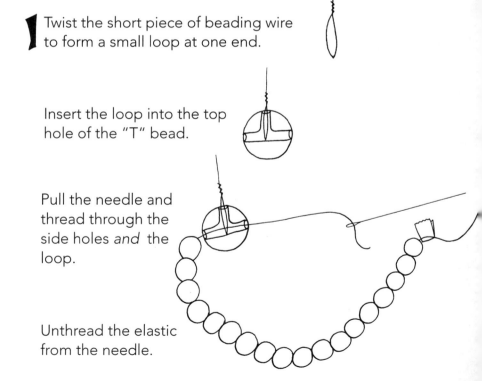

WHAT YOU NEED
12" (30 cm) of elastic thread
Tape
Beading needle
12-mm power beads (about 20)
3" (7.5 cm) beading wire, 30- or 34-gauge
"T" bead and cap bead (see next page)
Scissors

2 Snip off the tape, thread that end of the thread onto the needle, and pull it through the side holes and the loop.

Now, you have two threads going opposite ways through the bead.

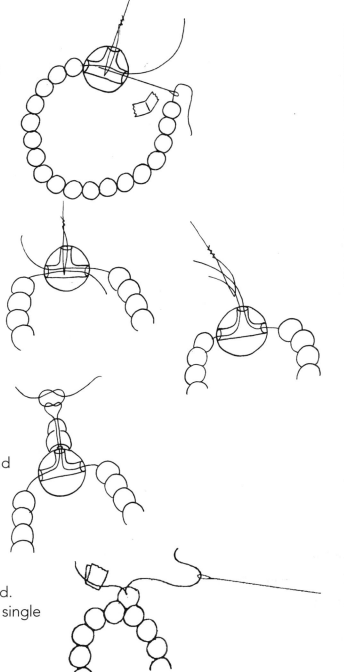

3 Very gently, pull the wire loop up out of the hole.

The loop will pull the two threads along with it.

To add a cap bead:

Feed the two threads through the cap bead and tie them in a lock knot* against the top.

To finish without a "T" bead:

Thread the needle through the first strung bead. This bead will stick up a little. Tie the ends in a single knot*. Or, finish off with a cap bead as above.

*See Techniques, pages 124–130.

"T" Beads and Cap Beads

The special finishing beads for power bead bracelets are not

*readily available in stores, and they don't even have standard names yet. I call one a **"T" bead** because it has three openings that form a "T". The **cap bead** is a smaller bead that sits on top of the "T" bead. The elastic goes through it and the knot sticks out the top.*

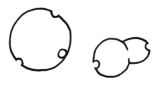

If you can't find these beads in stores, you can closely match your power bracelet's colors by making your own out of plastic clay (see page 14).

The Inside Scoop

Choosing the Right Thread

For a durable bracelet, use the thickest elastic thread that will fit through your beads. But remember, the thread also needs to fit through the eye of the needle. And on power bead bracelets, two widths of thread have to fit through the finishing beads.

Make-Your-Own POWER BEADS

Roll a small ball of plastic clay (like Sculpey) the size you want your bead to be. With a large needle, use a gentle drilling motion to make a hole in the center. Begin again on the other side directly across from the hole and "drill" until the two holes meet.

To make a "T" bead:

Add a third hole to form a T.

To make a cap bead:

Roll a small ball of clay, about half the size of your power beads. Roll out a slightly larger sphere. Put the smaller bead on top of the larger one and press together softly, rolling slightly to erase the join line.

With a large needle, use a gentle drilling motion to make a hole halfway down. Begin again at the bottom and "drill" until the two holes meet.

Bake beads according to the directions on the package of clay.

WILL YOUR BRACELET REALLY MAKE YOU SMARTER?

Writing an important report today? Wear a bracelet made with tiger's eye or gold beads for creativity! Some people believe that certain natural semiprecious stones and certain colors "empower" the wearer with special qualities. Just wearing these reminders can keep you on track — try it and see!

You can also use glass beads for your power beads. They often have much stronger colors than semiprecious stones — and are less expensive.

SEMIPRECIOUS STONES

Amethyst (violet): intelligence

Aventurine (pale green): success

Carnelian (red-orange): energy

Onyx (yellow-orange): self-control

Quartz (clear): clarity

Rose quartz (pink): love

Tiger's eye (yellow-brown): creativity

Turquoise (bright blue): health

COLORS

Black: stability, silence, endurance

Blue: dreams, friendship

Brown or Tan: confidence

Crimson: strength, courage

Deep blue: justice

Gold: creativity

Green: prosperity, growth

Indigo: harmony

Orange: healing, health, attraction

Pale violet: music, peace

Pink: love

Purple: leadership

Red: energy, purity

Silver: overcoming obstacles, protection

Turquoise: honor

White: intelligence, intuition

Yellow: joy, new beginnings

Imitation vs. Real Stones

When the price of a store-bought power bead bracelet seems too good to be true, the semiprecious stones are probably glass or plastic imitations. If you're happy with the look, then it doesn't matter that the stones aren't real. But one way to be sure you're using real stones is to make your own bracelets. Beads made of real semiprecious stones and minerals have great beauty and should be reasonably priced — you can make a power bead bracelet from them for about $5.

Blue Crystal Bracelet

T his easy-to-make bracelet offsets icy-cool clear beads with smaller deep blue crylstals for a sophisticated look. For an elegant alternative, use gold beads instead of the clear crystals.

1 Secure one end of the thread with a piece of tape; thread the other end through the needle. String on the beads, first one clear, then one blue.

2 Tie the ends with a lock knot*. Trim the threads.

WHAT YOU NEED

12" (30 cm) of elastic thread
Tape
Beading needle
7-mm clear glass beads (15)
4-mm cobalt blue crystal beads (15)
Scissors

See Techniques, pages 124–130.

CRYSTAL COLOR COMBOS

Try these other combinations of beads and crystals for special sparkle!

- *white freshwater pearls and deep green crystals*
- *bronze-tinted freshwater pearls and clear crystals*
- *little black glass beads and pink crystals*
- *pale pink beads and ruby red crystals*
- *aqua blue beads and sapphire blue crystals*
- *gold beads and clear crystals*

What is "Crystal"?

Crystal beads are made of a special glass. The most common type is "Austrian crystal." These glass beads from Austria are **faceted** (cut to have many surfaces so they reflect the light), which gives them their sparkle.

Even the lower grades of crystal can be expensive, so low-priced Austrian crystal jewelry in the stores is probably not genuine.

If you can't afford to do an entire bracelet of crystals, try spacing a few evenly between less expensive glass beads of a different color.

Fire polish beads *are a very glittery, less expensive substitute for crystals. These glass beads are also faceted, with rounder edges that catch the light. They come in more colors than crystal beads, and they shimmer with almost as much "fire."*

The Inside Scoop
Sharp Edges!

The facets on genuine crystals are very sharp, so watch out. The sharp edges have cut many a jewelry-maker's thread during the stringing!

Rhinestone & Seed Bead Multistrand Bracelet

This glittery little two-strand bracelet is easier than it looks. Purple seed beads are an especially good choice, because they enhance the highlights of the rhinestones.

Before you start:

Measure your wrist. Draw a line that's the same length on the paper, and center the two threads on this line. Experiment with placing the rhinestones along the thread until you get a look you like.

WHAT YOU NEED

Measuring tape
Pencil and paper
6" (15-cm) of thin stretchy monofilament (2)
30-mm pronged rhinestone back (3)
30-mm flat, faceted rhinestones (3)
Needle-nose pliers
Beading needle
Size 11 seed beads (enough to fill two strands around your wrist, about 150 beads), in the color of your choice
Crimp (2)

If you want all the rhinestones evenly spaced, be sure the distance between the outer rhinestones and the ends of the bracelet equals half the distance between the center rhinestone and an outer rhinestone as shown.

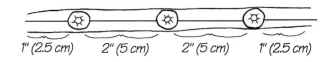

1" (2.5 cm)   2" (5 cm)   2" (5 cm)   1" (2.5 cm)

To make the bracelet:

1 Place the pronged back for the middle rhinestone behind the two threads where you want that stone. Place the rhinestone on top.

2 Press the prongs down with your fingers until the thread is held in place; then, tighten them with the pliers. If the threads slip, nudge them back into place with the needle. Be sure not to tighten too firmly, or the back will cut the elastic thread.

3 Thread the needle with one thread and string beads to where you're adding the next rhinestone. Repeat with the other thread.

4 Repeat steps 1 and 2 to attach the next rhinestone. Repeat step 3.

5 Attach the third rhinestone and fill the remainder of the strands with beads.

*See Techniques, pages 124–130.

6 Attach a crimp* to join one thread from each side. Be sure it's firm, but be careful not to press too hard, because you might cut the thread. Repeat with the remaining two threads.

MORE JAZZ!

String a Ring ... Make a mini-version using only one rhinestone.

... Or a Necklace! Cluster several rhinestones together on two beaded strands.

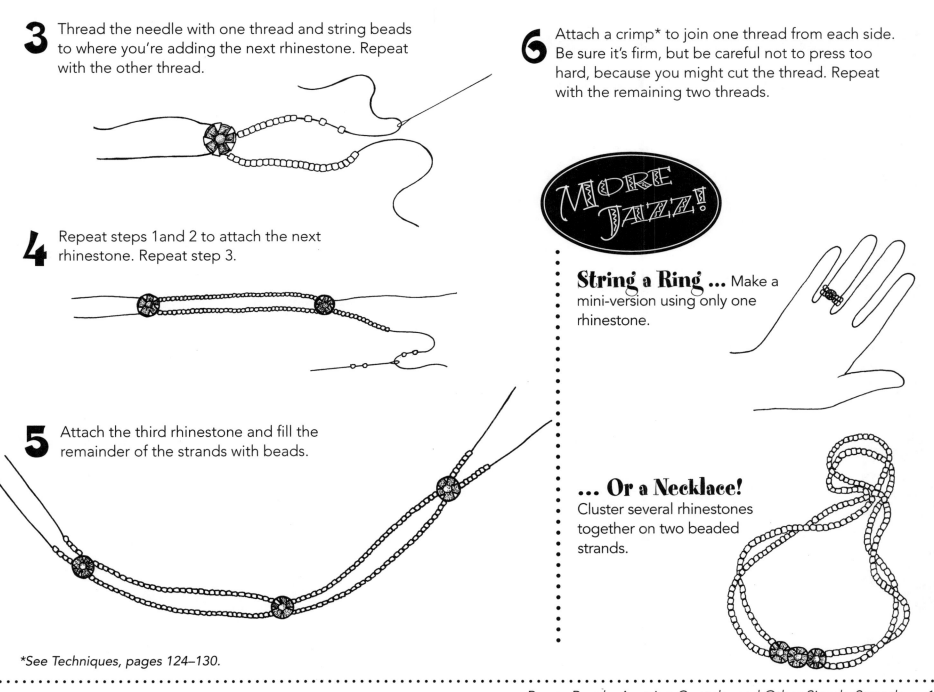

Double-Strand Butterfly Necklace

Now that you're a "super-strander," you're ready for two-hole beads! They're an easy way to create a more interesting look: The beaded strand looks as if it splits in two to pass through the two-hole bead, and then it merges back to one strand.

WHAT YOU NEED
28" (70 cm) of beading thread (2)
Tape
Beading needle (2)
Size 11 seed beads (enough to fill a 25" (62.5 cm) strand, about 500 beads)
Ruler or measuring tape
Two-hole butterfly or flower beads (3)
6-mm crystals (2)
Needle-nose pliers
Crimp (2)
Jump ring
Clasp

1 Holding the two threads together, secure the ends with a piece of tape. Thread both of the other ends through a needle.

String 4 1/2" (11 cm) of seed beads. Unthread one of the threads from the needle, and thread it through the other needle.

2 Now, follow this pattern for the double-strand section, passing both needles through the crystal.

Then unthread one needle, add that thread to the remaining needle, and string 4 1/2" (11 cm) of seed beads.

butterfly bead

crystal

butterfly bead

crystal

butterfly bead

1" (2.5 cm) seed beads

1/2" (1 cm) seed beads

1/2" (1 cm) seed beads

1" (2.5 cm) seed beads

4 1/2" (11 cm) inches seed beads

3 Attach a crimp* to each end to form a loop. Attach a clasp* to one loop and a jump ring* to the other loop.

The Inside Scoop
Using Two-Hole Beads

In a necklace, two-hole beads lie on an arc, so you might have to put a few more beads on the lower thread to make the beads lie smoothly.

*See Techniques, pages 124–130.

Spiral Danglers

For a new "twist" on stranding, let these spirals swing from your ears! They can be fancy or casual, depending on your bead selection. Use size 10 pretend pearls for a party look, or a mix of pastels for a fun-in-the-sun summery look.

WHAT YOU NEED
Eye pin (2)
Slender cylindrical object, like a pencil or chopstick
Beads (about 70, depending on the bead size and eye-pin length)
Needle-nose pliers
Scissors, nail clippers, or wire cutters
Ear wire (2)

*See Techniques, pages 124–130.

For each earring:

1 Holding an eye pin firmly against the cylinder with one hand, bend the straight part around the cylinder into a coil. Now, pull down on the coil to form a spiral.

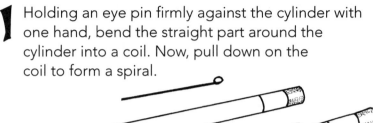

2 Slide on enough beads to cover the pin, leaving a little bit at the end. With the pliers, bend the end into a kink* and trim off any excess.

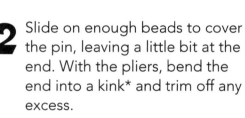

3 Slide the eye pin onto an ear wire and close it.

Pinch the ear wire to close it

Single-Strand Ring with Accent Pearl

You can have a real pearl ring for under $1! Single freshwater pearls (see page 33) come in many sizes. Some are tinted; others are naturally white. This ring uses iridescent black seed beads to offset the pearl.

1 Secure one end of the thread with a piece of tape; thread the other end through the needle. String half the beads. Add the pearl, and string the other half.

2 Check the length of the ring against your finger. When you're happy with the size, tie the ends together in a lock knot*. Trim the threads.

WHAT YOU NEED

8" (20 cm) of thin stretchy clear monofilament or thin elastic thread

Tape

Beading needle

Black iridescent seed beads (36 to 40)

4-mm freshwater pearl

Scissors

The Inside Scoop
Why So Much Thread?

For a ring, you need to start with a nice, long length of elastic or monofilament; shorter lengths are too difficult to work with when you're making such a small piece of jewelry.

RINGS

Double-Strand Ring with Power Bead

You can't wear too many power beads! This ring will look great with a power bead bracelet (see page 12).

1 Secure one end of the thread with a piece of tape; thread the other end through the needle.

2 String the power bead to the center of the thread. Add enough seed beads to fit a little snugly around your finger.

Bring the thread through the power bead to form the first loop.

WHAT YOU NEED
Tape
12" (30 cm) of thin clear stretchy monofilament or thin elastic thread
Beading needle
8-mm power bead
Seed beads (about 60, depending on finger size), in the color of your choice
Scissors

3 Add half the number of seed beads that are on the first loop.

Remove the needle and secure the beads with a piece of tape around the thread.

4 Remove the other piece of tape; thread the needle onto this end of the thread. String with the other half of the beads.

5 Tie the thread with a lock knot*. Trim the ends.

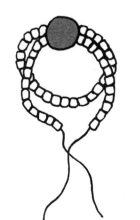

See Techniques, pages 124–130.

Triple-Strand Ring with Coil Bead

*W*ith their large holes and bright, shiny colors, coil beads are a fun way to join multistrands for a different look.

1 Secure one end of the thread with a piece of tape; thread the other end through the needle. String on the coil bead, pulling it about two-thirds of the way down the strand. Add as many seed beads as it takes to fit your finger snugly.

2 Bring the needle through the coil bead again, forming the first strand.

3 String the same number of seed beads and bring the needle through the coil bead to form the second strand.

WHAT YOU NEED
12" (30 cm) of elastic thread
Tape
Beading needle
Coil bead
Seed beads (approximately 75 to 80)
Scissors

4 String on half the number of beads and secure them with tape.

5 Remove the tape on the other thread; thread the needle onto it. String on the remaining beads.

6 Tie the ends together with a lock knot*. Trim the threads.

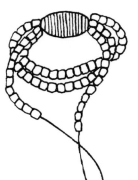

See Techniques, pages 124–130.

Coil Beads

Coil beads are just that: beads shaped out of a tiny coil of slender wire. They look just like miniature springs, so they're also called **spring beads**. They come in all kinds of interesting shapes from barrels to slender tubes. Made out of a specially treated aluminum, they are available in amazing colors like brilliant pink, green, and blue. Coil beads are a little pricey (50 cent and up), but you only need one for a striking effect on a ring.

The Savvy Bead Buyer

Beaded Tension Clips

A few seed beads can jazz up an ordinary hair clip in no time and put some sparkle in your hair! Seed beads come in a rainbow of colors, so make a pair to match every outfit.

1 Push one end of the beading wire through the small hole at the top of the tension clip and wrap it around the clip three or four times. Tuck the end under the wrapped section to secure it.

2 Slide on enough beads to cover the width of the clip.

WHAT YOU NEED
Tension hair clip (1 pair)
36" (90 cm) of 34-gauge beading wire
Seed beads (about 120), in the color of your choice
Scissors, nail clippers, or wire cutters

Wrap the beaded section around the clip, bringing the wire up the other side.

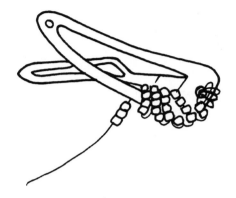

Continue like this, adding beads and wrapping the wire, until you've covered the entire clip and are back at the hole.

3 Push the wire through the hole and secure it, as you did in step 1. Snip off the excess wire.

A Touch of Elegance. Wire a crystal bead or a freshwater pearl to the head of the clip.

Yipes! Stripes! Try varying bead colors to make stripes. Or, alternate four or five shades of the same color seed bead to create a shimmery effect.

Beaded Tieback

Can an elastic hair tieback be a fashion accessory? Sure — when you decorate it with your favorite beads! Use a mixture, including a few tiny teardrops or semiprecious stone chips for color.

1 Twist one end of the wire around the tieback several times near the metal crimp, bringing it under the prior loops to secure it.

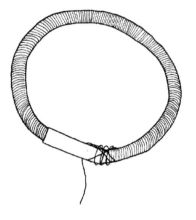

2 Slide the beads onto the wire, interspersing the accent beads along the strand. Now, wrap the wire around the hair tieback, covering the metal crimp.

3 Wrap the end of the wire around the tieback several times; then, pull the end through the loops to secure it. Snip off the excess wire.

WHAT YOU NEED

18" (45 cm) of 34-gauge beading wire

Elastic hair tieback

Seed beads (about 50), in a mix of colors

Small accent beads (3 to 4)

Scissors, nail clippers, or wire cutters

"Beady" Creatures and Charms

Dragonflies, ladybugs, flowers, stars, tiny bows — here are all your favorite beaded creatures and shapes to sparkle as you step! To make these "beadies," you simply shape a beaded strand of wire or use the easy "double-weave" technique (remember the Beady Buddy craze?). Then, attach them to earrings, rings, and necklaces. Weave them into bracelets. Wire them onto your bobby pins, clips, and combs. Dangle them from your backpack or key chain. In other words, wear them wherever you want some color and flash!

Flower & Pearl Hair Pin

How difficult? Easy!
Time: 30 minutes

The pin disappears in your hair, leaving this flower magically "floating."

1 Slide 20 beads onto the wire. Bend the beaded section into a petal shape and twist the base to secure it.

2 Repeat, adding 20 beads each time, to form four more petals. Spread them out into a flower shape.

3 Bring one end of the wire up between two petals and slide on the three pearls. Center them on the flower so that they conceal the twisted bases.

4 Bend both wire ends around to the back of the flower and use them to fasten the flower onto the bobby pin.

WHAT YOU NEED
Seed beads (100), in the color of your choice
10" (25 cm) of 22- or 24-gauge beading wire
3-mm pretend pearls (3)
Bobby pin

Want a Larger Flower? If you've got thick or very curly hair, try a bigger, more dramatic flower. Use a 12" (30 cm) length of wire, about 140 seed beads, and a 7-mm crystal of a contrasting color or one pretend pearl as a finishing touch. Wire the flower to a larger bobby pin or a hair comb.

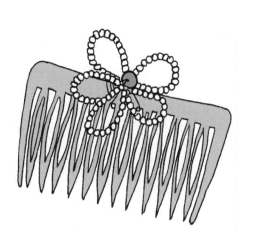

Pearls

*If you love the look of pearls, you can really go wild with the plastic ones, also called **pretend** or **faux** (foe) pearls. They come in a variety of sizes — and you can buy a big bucket of them for about $1!*

*Real **freshwater**, or **natural**, pearls start at about 50 cents apiece, so use them sparingly — as a special accent bead, for example (see Single-Strand Ring with Accent Pearl, page 23). In addition to their natural ivory color, they come in wonderful shades of pale pink, purple, gold, and shiny black.*

HAIR COMBS

Hair combs are, without a doubt, the most versatile hair ornament. Inexpensive plastic combs come four or six to a pack, so share a package among friends. Use them to smooth the sides of a ponytail, to hold a side part, to sweep back hair to show off your earrings, or to decorate a French twist. And, of course, you'll want to embellish them with beadies first!

Delicate Dragonfly

𝕋his airy dragonfly alights on a bobby pin or a clip. Silver-lined beads and shiny black-green seed beads are perfect for creating a dragonfly's natural iridescent flash.

WHAT YOU NEED

Black-green opalescent seed beads (48)
15" (37.5 cm) of 22- or 24-gauge beading wire
4-mm black bead
Silver-lined blue seed beads (104)
5-mm pale blue crystal
Needle-nose pliers
Scissors, nail clippers, or wire cutters

To form the body:

1 Slide 32 of the black-green seed beads onto the wire. Fold the wire in half so there are 16 beads on each side.

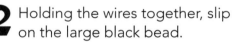

Twist it gently three times so it looks like this:

2 Holding the wires together, slip on the large black bead.

To form the lower wings:

3 Spread the unbeaded wires out to each side. Slide 20 blue seed beads onto one wire, form a loop, and twist the wing to "lock" it.

Repeat on the other side.

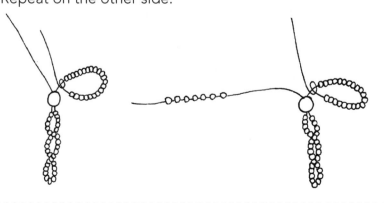

To form the upper wings:

4 Move the right wire to the left side and the left wire to the right side.

Add 32 blue beads to one wire, form a loop, and twist the wing to "lock" it. Repeat on the other side.

To form the head:

5 Slide three black-green beads onto each wire to make the neck. Then, holding the wires together, slide on the blue crystal for the head. Slide five black-green beads onto each wire to form antennae. Kink* the ends; then snip off the excess wire.

See Techniques, pages 124–130.

ATTACHING YOUR BEADIES

You'll never run out of places to show off your beadies! The ones shaped out of a strand of beading wire are more delicate — they're perfect for decorating hair accessories like pins and combs, for example, but won't hold up as zipper pulls. You can put those sturdy little double-weave beadies just about anywhere, however.

If you want your beady firmly attached:

Wire it on with narrow (34-gauge) beading wire.

If you want your beady to dangle:

Wire on a jump ring.

Shining Star Charm

W̱ith just a little practice, you can turn out a whole constellation of these tiny stars in under a hour.

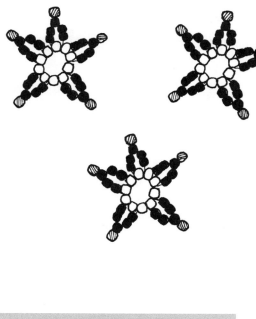

How difficult? Moderate
Time: 15 minutes

To form the center of the star:

1 Secure one end of the thread with a piece of tape; thread the other end through the needle. String the gold beads. Pull the needle and thread through the first bead you strung on, forming a loop.

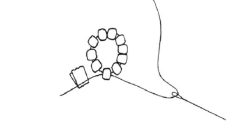

Tie the thread to the loop with a lock knot*.

WHAT YOU NEED
12" (30 cm) of beading thread
Tape
Beading needle
Size 11 gold beads (10)
Size 11 deep blue beads (25)
Size 11 silver beads (5)
Scissors

*See Techniques, pages 124–130.

continued next page

CHARMS

To form each star "point":

2 Follow these two steps:

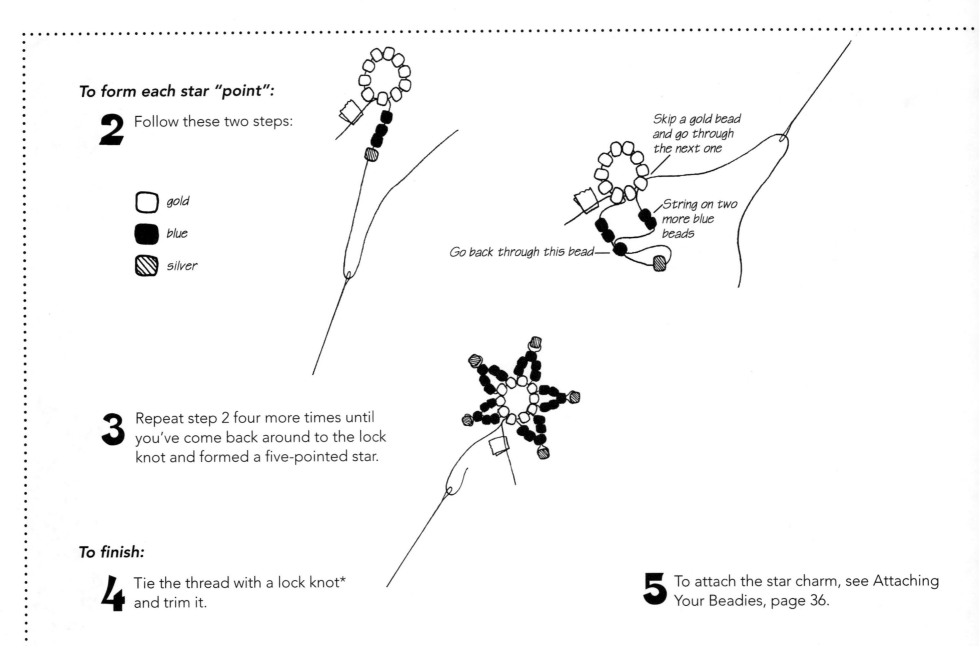

gold

blue

silver

Skip a gold bead and go through the next one

String on two more blue beads

Go back through this bead

3 Repeat step 2 four more times until you've come back around to the lock knot and formed a five-pointed star.

To finish:

4 Tie the thread with a lock knot* and trim it.

5 To attach the star charm, see Attaching Your Beadies, page 36.

Stars A-Dangling. Wire a jump ring (see Attaching Your Beadies, page 36) to the top bead of a star point and slip the ring through an ear wire. Repeat for a pair of starry earrings.

Starry, Starry Night. How about a sprinkle of silvery or pearl stars along the scoop neckline of a black T-shirt? Takes only minutes to stitch them on!

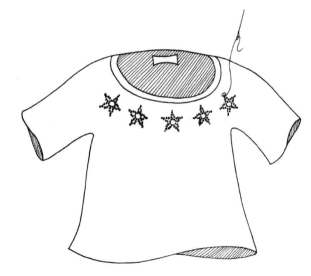

The Inside Scoop
Passing through a Bead Twice

Check the hole before you string on the bead to be sure it's nice and even, so the double thickness of thread can fit through easily.

Sunburst Charm

There's nothing like wearing a little piece of sunshine to make you feel good!

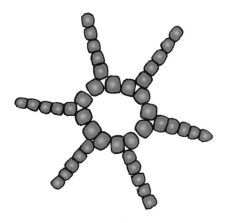

WHAT YOU NEED

10" (25 cm) of beading thread
Tape
Beading needle
Gold seed beads (42)
Scissors

To form the center of the sun:

1 Secure one end of the thread with a piece of tape; thread the other end through the needle. String 12 beads. Pull the needle and thread through the first bead you strung on, forming a loop.

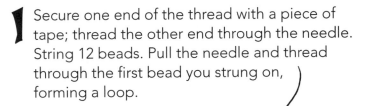

Go through the first bead again from the opposite side

Tie the thread to the loop with a lock knot*.

*See Techniques, pages 124–130.

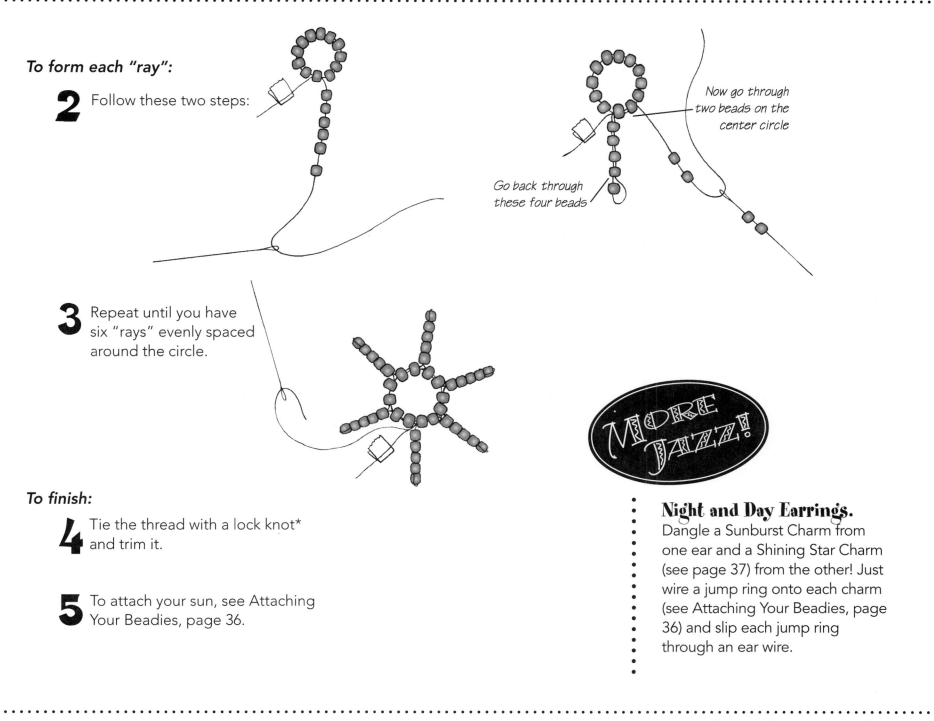

To form each "ray":

2 Follow these two steps:

Now go through two beads on the center circle

Go back through these four beads

3 Repeat until you have six "rays" evenly spaced around the circle.

To finish:

4 Tie the thread with a lock knot* and trim it.

5 To attach your sun, see Attaching Your Beadies, page 36.

MORE JAZZ!

Night and Day Earrings.
Dangle a Sunburst Charm from one ear and a Shining Star Charm (see page 37) from the other! Just wire a jump ring onto each charm (see Attaching Your Beadies, page 36) and slip each jump ring through an ear wire.

"Beady" Bumblebee Charm

How difficult? Moderate
Time: 30 minutes

Double-weave a tiny striped bee! The iridescent beads (see page 35) give it just the right sparkle and flash.

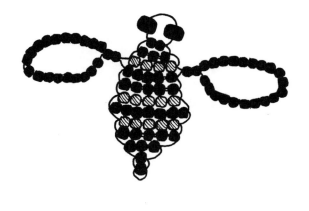

WHAT YOU NEED

24" (60 cm) of 34-gauge beading or brass wire

Size 6 black beads (2)

Iridescent black seed beads (74)

Bright yellow seed beads (14)

Scissors, nail clippers, or wire cutters

To form the head:

1 Make a loop with the wire. Slide one size 6 black bead onto each end of the wire. Slide two black seed beads onto one wire and double-weave (see Do the Double Weave!, page 44) them.

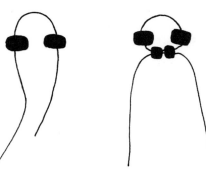

To start the body:

2 Double-weave the seed beads as shown:

 black

yellow

To form the wings:

3 Slide 21 black seed beads onto one wire. Push the wire back through the first two seed beads as shown to form a loop.

Repeat on the other side.

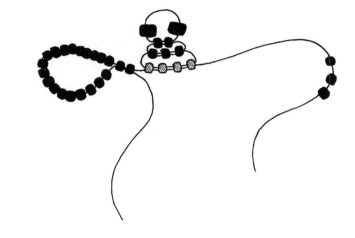

To finish the body and make the stinger:

4 Double-weave the seed beads in this pattern:

■ black

▨ yellow

5 To finish the ends, see page 45.

6 To attach your bumblebee charm, see Attaching Your Beadies, page 36.

LIKE THE DOUBLE-WEAVE LOOK?

Check out the lattice jewelry on pages 110–121 that uses the same technique for elegant chokers and rings in beautiful colors and styles of beads!

DO THE DOUBLE WEAVE!

If you've made Beady Buddies, you're an old pro at double-weaving. If not, it'll take you only a minute or two to get the hang of it. Let's say you're going to double-weave a four-bead-wide strip:

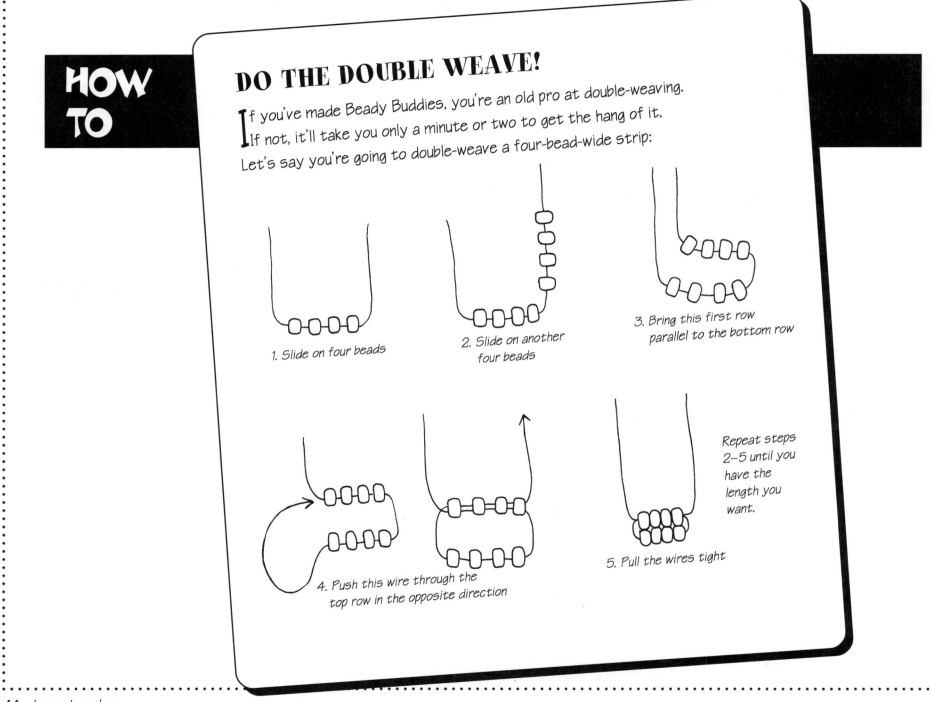

1. Slide on four beads

2. Slide on another four beads

3. Bring this first row parallel to the bottom row

4. Push this wire through the top row in the opposite direction

5. Pull the wires tight

Repeat steps 2–5 until you have the length you want.

DOUBLE WEAVING continued

Illustrations for double-weave patterns typically look like this one. It's showing you how many beads and what color to use for each row.

The finished "beady" will look like this.

To finish the ends:

Weave the wires back through the last two rows

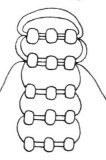

Wrap them around the wires on the edges

Trim them and tuck in the ends

If you're making a ring (pages 116-120), form the double-weave strip into a loop and join the first and last rows as shown.

Then finish the ends as shown above.

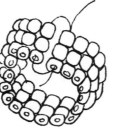

The Inside Scoop
Seed Bead Tips

Misshapen seed beads will give a lumpy, uneven result to your weaving, so pick through your beads to be sure you choose ones with a uniform size and shape.

If size 11 seed beads are difficult for you to handle comfortably, try a larger size, such as 8 or 6.

"Beady" Dragonfly Charm

Here's a slightly different style of beaded dragonfly from the one on page 34 — perfect for dangling!

To form the head and eyes:

1 Slide one black seed bead, the crystal, and the other black bead to the center of the wire.

WHAT YOU NEED
Black iridescent seed beads (2)
5-mm blue or green crystal
24" (60 cm) of 34-gauge beading or brass wire
Silver-lined green seed beads (126)
Scissors, nail clippers, or wire cutters

2 Double-weave (see Do the Double Weave!, page 44) three rows as shown:

⊗ crystal

▨ black

▦ green

To form the first set of wings:

3 Slide 25 green seed beads onto one wire. Pull the wire through the first bead as shown to form a loop.

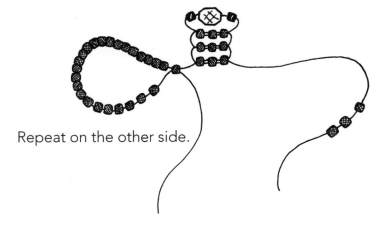

Repeat on the other side.

To form the second set of wings:

4 Double-weave one row of three green beads. Then, slide on 20 seed beads and form a wing. Repeat on the other side.

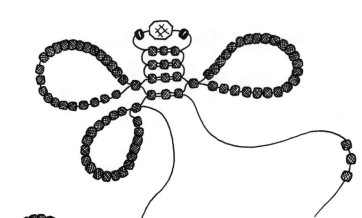

To form the tail:

5 Double-weave one row of three green beads. Double-weave 10 rows of two green beads followed by one row of one green bead as shown:

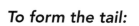

6 To finish the ends, see page 45.

7 To attach your dragonfly charm, see Attaching Your Beadies, page 36.

The Inside Scoop
Brass Wire

Readily available at the hardware store for only pennies a foot, brass wire is more flexible than beading wire. You'll find it easier to work with, especially when you're new to double weaving.

Fish-Round-Your-Wrist "Beady" Bracelet

How difficult? More challenging
Time: 1 hour

These tiny fish are perfect for summer outfits and the swimming season! You can use all one color (orange or yellow beads to make a tiny goldfish, for example) or follow the pattern here for a tropical splash!

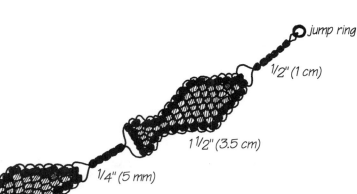

jump ring

1/2" (1 cm)

1 1/2" (3.5 cm)

1/4" (5 mm)

1 1/2" (3.5 cm)

1/4" (5 mm)

1 1/2" (3.5 cm)

1/2" (1 cm)

clasp

This bracelet will fit a 6" (15 cm) wrist. Measuring each section of your bracelet as you work will ensure a good fit.

WHAT YOU NEED

Measuring tape
Jump ring (2)
3' (90 cm) of 34-gauge beading or brass wire
Size 11 black seed beads (about 140)
Size 11 orange seed beads, (about 125)
Seed bead in contrasting color for eye (3)
Tweezers
Scissors, nail clippers, or wire cutters
Clasp

To make the bracelet:

1 Slide a jump ring onto the middle of the wire; fold the wire in half. Slide 1/4" (5 mm) of black beads over both ends of the doubled wire to form the first section of beaded strand.

2 Gently separate the wires. Slide two black beads onto one wire. Now, double-weave (see Do the Double Weave!, page 44) the fish shown here:

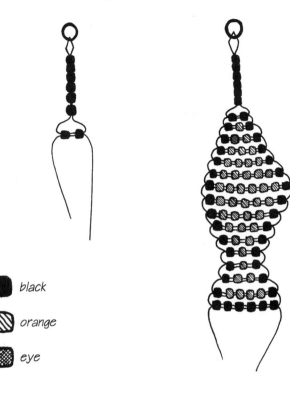

▪ black

▨ orange

▦ eye

3 Hold the wires together and slide on 1/4" (5 mm) of the black beads as shown in step 1. Repeat the pattern until your bracelet looks like the drawing on page 48 (without the jump ring and clasp).

*See Techniques, pages 124–130.

4 Use the remaining wire to attach a jump ring*. Attach a clasp* to one end of the bracelet.

Forever Blowing Bubbles!
Before you slide on the first two beads of the double-weave pattern, slide on a crystal at the opening of each fish's mouth as shown.

RUNNING OUT OF WIRE?
It's easier to double-weave with a shorter length of wire, but you may not have enough to finish your bracelet. No problem! Just cut a 2' (60 cm) length, slide it through the row you just finished and continue double-weaving. When you've finished the piece of jewelry, finish the ends of the first section of wire (see page 45).

Circle-of-Ladybugs "Beady" Bracelet

Spin a merry-go-round of ladybugs — the bug that's all the rage — around your wrist.

This bracelet will fit a 6" (15 cm) wrist. Measuring each section of your bracelet as you work will ensure a good fit.

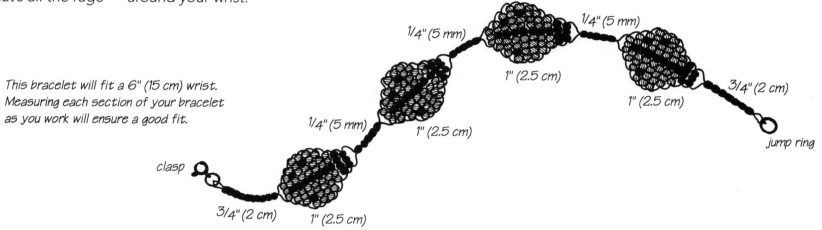

1/4" (5 mm)

1/4" (5 mm)

1" (2.5 cm)

3/4" (2 cm)

jump ring

1" (2.5 cm)

1/4" (5 mm)

1" (2.5 cm)

clasp

3/4" (2 cm)

1" (2.5 cm)

WHAT YOU NEED

Measuring tape
Jump ring (2)
3' (90 cm) of 34-gauge beading or brass wire
Size 11 black seed beads (about 100)
Size 11 red seed beads (about 180)
Tweezers
Scissors, nail clippers, or wire cutters
Clasp

To make the bracelet:

1 Slide a jump ring onto the middle of the wire; fold the wire in half. Slide 3/4" (2 cm) of black beads onto both ends of the doubled wire to form the first section of beaded strand.

2 Gently separate the wires. Slide two black beads onto one end of the wire, and double-weave (see Do the Double Weave!, page 44) a ladybug shown here:

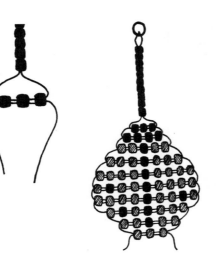

▪ black
▨ red

3 Hold the wires together and slide on 1/4" (1 cm) of black beads as shown in step 1. Follow step 2 to make another ladybug. Then, repeat the pattern until your bracelet looks like the drawing on page 50 (without the jump ring and clasp).

4 Use the remaining wire to attach a jump ring*. Attach a clasp* to one end of the bracelet.

*See Techniques, pages 124–130.

MORE "BEADY" MAGIC: EARRINGS TO MATCH

How about a matching pair of earrings? You can use these double-weave charm patterns to make just the beady charm and then dangle it wherever you like!

Start with an 18" (45 cm) length of beading wire. Follow the double-weave pattern for the charm you want to make: fish or ladybug. Finish the ends (see page 45); then see Attaching your Beadies, page 36.

WANT A LONGER BRACELET?

Or how about an anklet? Easy! Just make the straight sections longer.

Here's a handy guide to help you determine how many size 11 beads to add:

5 seed beads = 1/4" (5 mm)
10 seed beads = 1/2" (1 cm)

Beaded Bow-Tie Earrings

Once you get the hang of these tiny charming bows, you'll be able to whip up a pair in minutes. They're so cute you'll want to use them in lots of ways (in addition to gift wrapping your ears!).

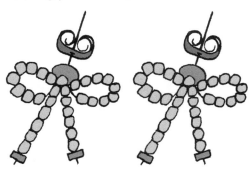

WHAT YOU NEED
10" (25 cm) of beading thread (2)
Tape
Beading needle
Seed beads (66), in the color of your choice
Crimp (4)
Needle-nose pliers
Scissors, nail clippers, or wire cutters
Strong glue*
Ear post with small disk (2)
Ear nut (2)

***Note: You'll need a grown-up's help to use this type of glue; please see page 134 before starting.**

How difficult? Moderate
Time: 10 minutes per bow tie
(faster with practice)

To make each bow tie:

1 Secure one end of the thread with a piece of tape; thread the other end through the needle. String 17 seed beads and slide them onto the middle of the thread.

Draw the needle back through the seventh bead you strung on (now called the "middle bead") from the direction shown.

You just formed a beaded loop and the first bow "tail."

2 String 10 more beads. Make another loop, passing through the same middle bead again as shown.

String six beads.

3 Attach a crimp* just below the beads on each "tail." Trim the threads below the crimps. Add a drop of glue on each end to be sure the thread doesn't pull out.

After the glue is dry, fiddle with the bow tie until the shape hangs nicely.

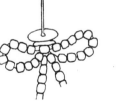

To attach the ear post:

4 Place the bow tie on a flat surface.

If your ear post disk is solid, apply a thin layer of glue to the disk. Press the bow against the disk.

Let the glue cure completely.

If your ear post disk has perforations, attach it to the bow with wire or thread.

See Techniques, pages 124–130.

MORE JAZZ!

Transform Your Tanks and Ts. Decorate the scoop necklines of your favorite summer shirts with these tiny bows. Just sew on a couple of beads in the loop and let the ends dangle.

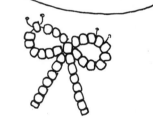

"Tie Up" Your Hair. To wire the bows onto bobby pins for a delicate line of beaded bows in your hair, see Attaching Your Beadies, page 36.

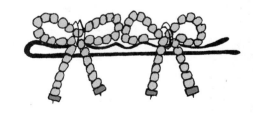

Crazy Daisy Dangles

The perfect earrings to celebrate the arrival of spring — or to lift your spirits on a dreary winter day.

WHAT YOU NEED
8" (20 cm) of 4-lb (1.85-kg) monofilament
(2) Tape
Beading needle
Size 8 white seed beads (14)
Size 8 yellow seed beads (2)
Size 11 green seed beads (14)
Jump ring (2)
Scissors
Ear wire (2)

To make each earring:

1 Secure one end of the monofilament with a piece of tape; thread the other through the needle. String seven white seed beads. Pass the needle through the first bead you strung, being careful to enter it from the direction shown, so the beads form a loop.

2 String a yellow seed bead. Bring the monofilament across the circle so that the yellow bead is in the center. Now, pass the monofilament through a white bead as shown.

See how you've formed a daisy?

3 Add seven green seed beads.

Pass the monofilament through a jump ring

Now go back through the green beads

Tie the thread onto the circle with a lock knot* and trim it

4 Slip the jump ring into the ear wire as shown and close it. Remove the tape and knot the "tail" of the monofilament with a lock knot*.

Pinch the ear wire to close it

The Inside Scoop
While You're Beading ...

Pour the beads you're using onto white paper plates or into yougurt lids or shallow light-colored bowls. You can see all the colors, and the beads will be easy to get at.

*See Techniques, pages 124–130.

The Best Five-Petal Flower Ring

This ring uses the same technique as the Beaded Bow-Tie Earrings (see page 52) to form five loops. Just as you are wondering how the petals are going to come together, suddenly, with one little twist, it's a flower!

WHAT YOU NEED
Seed beads for the flower (55), in the color of your choice
12" (30 cm) of 34-gauge beading wire
Seed beads for the ring (about 25, depending on finger size), in an alternate color
4- or 5-mm crystal or other accent bead
Scissors, nail clippers, or wire cutters
Tweezers

To form the flower:

1 Slide on 11 beads about three-fourths of the way down the wire. Push one end of the wire through the first bead you strung on (now called the "middle bead") as shown to make the first petal's loop.

The Inside Scoop

No Droopy Petals!

Using wire instead of thread creates a flower that will hold its perfectly shaped petals. Beading thread will stretch and loosen over time, causing the petals to droop.

2 On the longer side of the wire, slide on 11 more beads and make another loop by passing through a new "middle bead" as described in step 1.

Repeat until you have a total of five petals.

4 Slide the crystal bead onto the longer wire. To position the crystal in the center of the flower, bring that wire up between two petals and then down between two petals on the other side.

Now, slide the shorter wire through the crystal.

3 Twist the two ends of the wire together to close the petals into a circle, forming a flower.

continued next page

To make the ring:

5 Fill both wires with an equal number of beads, enough to fasten around your finger.

6 Twist the ends of the wires together twice, so the beads are held snug against each other. Hide the ends on each side as shown:

Trim excess wire.

Rainbow Petals. To create an accent of color in each petal, use a different color bead to start each string of 10 beads.

Floating-on-Air Illusions

The magic of illusion jewelry is the way the beads and charms appear to float around your throat or lie scattered in your hair. The trick to this "invisible" look is to use a special clear stringing material. You can create all the popular necklaces and hair accessories (plus create your own style!) just by varying the number of strands, spacing the beads evenly or scattering them irregularly, and suspending one or more special charms.

THE ILLUSION TECHNIQUE

To create the effect that your beads are "floating," you string them on *monofilament* (also sold as illusion cord), which comes in a fantastic stretchy version, too. Stretchy monofilament is the most expensive of all the strand materials, but this stuff is so fun and easy to work with (no clasp needed — just crimp the ends together and you're finished!), plus it lies flat and won't kink. You'll find two weights: thick and thin. The regular (nonstretchy) beading monofilament (sold by weight) also costs a bit more, but it's quality stuff, too.

You can also use *fishing line* from a hardware or sporting goods store, and a few dollars' worth will stretch to the moon and back. Check it out — you'll get hooked!

Butterfly Pendant Illusion Necklace

Catch this pretty butterfly bead on the wing to celebrate spring!

How difficult? Easy!
Time: 45 minutes

1 Slide the seed bead that matches your butterfly bead to the center of the monofilament. Slip the butterfly bead over both ends of the doubled strand so it hangs as a pendant.

WHAT YOU NEED

Seed bead, in the color of your choice

Butterfly bead with an up-and-down hole, in the same color as the single seed bead

20" (50 cm) of 4-lb (1.85-kg) clear monofilament

Seed beads (26), in the color of your choice

5-mm crystals (2), in the color of your choice

Crimp (2)

Needle-nose pliers

Clasp

Jump ring

2 Slide 13 beads and a crystal onto each end of the monofilament.

3 Attach a crimp to form a loop* in each end of the monofilament and attach a clasp* to one end of the necklace.

See Techniques, pages 124–130.

NECKLACES

Stretchy Pearl Illusion Necklace

This simple but elegant circle of floating natural pearls (see page 33) is so quick and easy to create — a perfect last-minute gift that you made!

1 Draw a 2¹/₂" (6 cm) line on the foam board or paper.

2 Slide the first pearl to the center of the strand. Tie a lock knot* on each side of the pearl.

WHAT YOU NEED

Pencil
Piece of foam board or paper
Ruler or measuring tape
30" (75 cm) of thin stretchy clear monofilament
5-mm natural pearls (9)
Crimp
Scissors
Needle-nose pliers

The Inside Scoop
Stringing the Pearls

The pearls' holes are small, so coax the beads along and handle the strand gently. You don't want to stretch it so tightly that it breaks.

See Techniques, pages 124–130.

3 Working from side to side, use your line as a reference to attach the remaining pearls following this pattern:

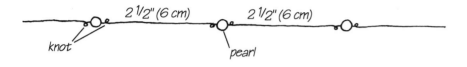

knot

2 1/2" (6 cm)   2 1/2" (6 cm)

pearl

4 To finish, slide both ends of the monofilament through the crimp. In the mirror, adjust the length of the necklace. Attach the crimp*.

MORE JAZZ!

More than an Illusion! Instead of the invisible look, show off your pearls by stringing them on Nymo or Nylux. These special silky nylon beading threads come in very rich colors like purple, pink, or gold that almost glow in intensity.

The Inside Scoop
Checking Your Measurements

For spacing beads at regular intervals along a strand, a line drawn on foam board or on paper, rather than a ruler, is a quicker, easier way to check a measurement. Try it — you'll see!

Triple-Star Illusion Necklace

$Silver stars surround shiny, diamond-cut glass sparklers for your own personal constellation.

How difficult? Easy!
Time: 15 minutes

1 Hold one end of each strand together. Attach a crimp to form a loop* in the ends.

2 Attach a jump ring* to each star charm and slide one charm onto each strand.

3 Gather the ends together. Holding the necklace around your neck, look in the mirror to see if you like where each star hangs. Adjust to your taste by shortening or lengthening any of the uncrimped strands. Then, holding the strands together at those lengths, attach a crimp to form a loop* in the ends. Trim the ends of monofilament if necessary. Add a clasp* to one end of the necklace and a jump ring* to the other end.

See Techniques, pages 124–130.

WHAT YOU NEED
16" (40 cm), 18" (45 cm), and 20" (50 cm) of 4-lb (1.85-kg) clear monofilament
Crimp (2)
Needle-nose pliers
Jump ring (3)
Silver star charms with a faceted glass insert, typically sold in a package (3)
Scissors
Clasp
Jump ring

Pearl & Seed Bead Illusion Necklace

How difficult? Moderate
Time: 45 minutes

*Y̨ou can have a real pearl necklace for well under $5 using 5-mm **freshwater**, also called **natural**, pearls (see page 33). The **opalescent** seed beads (see page 35) offset the natural luster and charming individual shapes of the pearls.*

1 Draw a 2" (5 cm) line on the foam board or paper.

WHAT YOU NEED

Pencil
Piece of foam board or paper
Ruler or measuring tape
16" (40 cm) of thin stretchy clear monofilament
Tape
Beading needle
Black opalescent seed beads (7)
5-mm rose-tone freshwater pearls (7)
Crimp
Needle-nose pliers
Scissors

*See Techniques, pages 124–130.

2 Secure one end of the monofilament with a piece of tape; thread the other end through the needle. String one seed bead and one pearl onto the strand and gently work them along to the center. Now, pull the monofilament back through the bottom of the seed bead so it sits on top of the pearl.

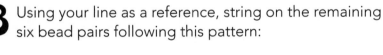

3 Using your line as a reference, string on the remaining six bead pairs following this pattern:

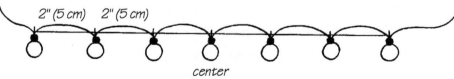

2" (5 cm)   2" (5 cm)

center

4 Hold the ends of the strand together and slip on the crimp. Holding the necklace around your neck, look in the mirror to adjust the length of the necklace to your own taste. Then, holding the ends at that length, attach a crimp*. Trim the ends of the monofilament if necessary.

Stretchy Rhinestone Illusion Necklace

Suspend *tiny sparks of light against your throat with this simple necklace — the look is amazing!*

WHAT YOU NEED

Pencil
Piece of foam board or paper
Ruler or measuring tape
16" (40 cm) of thin stretchy clear monofilament
Pronged rhinestone back (3 or more)
30-mm flat, faceted rhinestones (3 or more)
Needle-nose pliers
Crimp
Scissors

1 Draw a line the length of your monofilament on the foam board or paper. Use your ruler or measuring tape to mark it as shown.

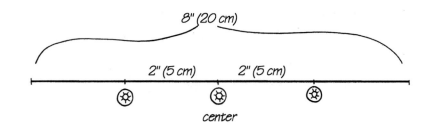

2 Lay the monofilament along your line. At the center, slip a pronged back under the monofilament.

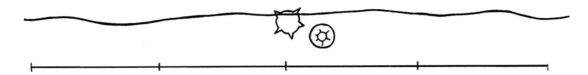

Place one rhinestone into the backing. Press the prongs down with your fingers until the monofilament is held in place; then, tighten with pliers.

Be careful not to tighten too firmly, or the back will cut the monofilament.

Repeat to add the remaining rhinestones.

3 Slide the ends of the monofilament through the crimp. Now, experiment with the length (see The Inside Scoop, right). Be sure the necklace stretches easily over your head. When you have the length you want, attach the crimp*. Trim the ends of the monofilament if necessary.

See Techniques, pages 124–130.

The Inside Scoop
Dangling Rhinestones

You want these rhinestones to dangle without flipping up. So, the necklace should fit closely, but not *too* tightly around your neck, and be sure to position the monofilament against the prongs as shown in step 2.

Shooting Star Illusion Necklace

G̲littering seed beads make the perfect "trail" for this tiny shooting star.

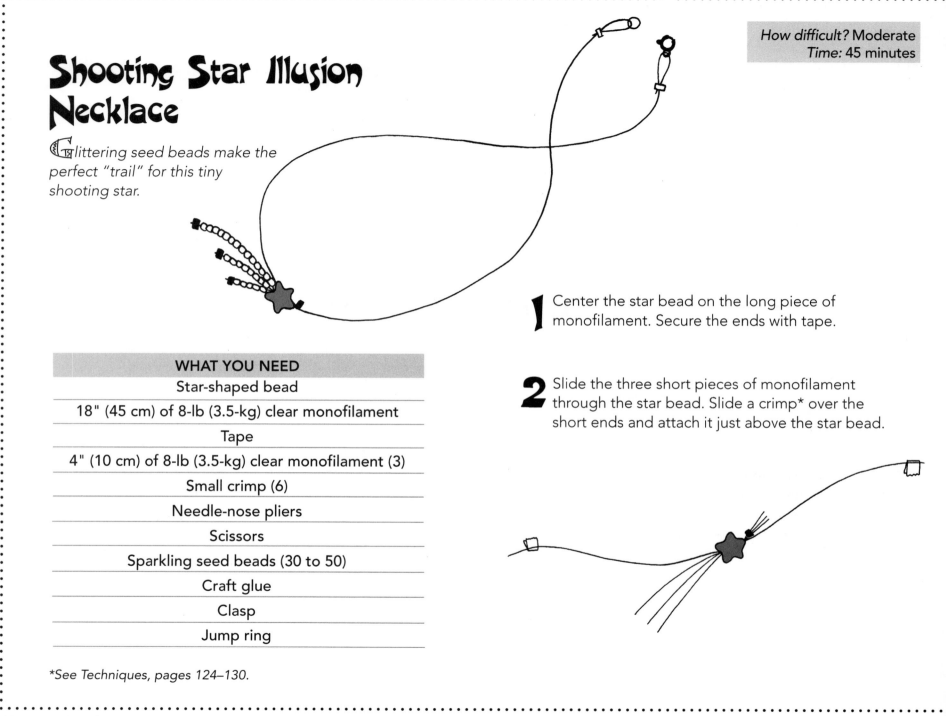

WHAT YOU NEED
Star-shaped bead
18" (45 cm) of 8-lb (3.5-kg) clear monofilament
Tape
4" (10 cm) of 8-lb (3.5-kg) clear monofilament (3)
Small crimp (6)
Needle-nose pliers
Scissors
Sparkling seed beads (30 to 50)
Craft glue
Clasp
Jump ring

*See Techniques, pages 124–130.

1 Center the star bead on the long piece of monofilament. Secure the ends with tape.

2 Slide the three short pieces of monofilament through the star bead. Slide a crimp* over the short ends and attach it just above the star bead.

3 To create the shooting star "tail," fill each short strand with a different number of seed beads and attach a crimp* firmly against the last bead on each strand.

Clip the strands as shown:

4 Remove the tape from the long monofilament. Attach a crimp to form a loop* in each end of the monofilament. Attach a clasp* to one end and a jump ring* to the other end of the necklace.

Add a drop of glue to each crimp on the star "tail" to secure it and let them dry.

Get Caught in a "Meteor Shower"!
Intersperse several twinkly star beads with the seed beads on the short pieces of monofilament.

Sport Your Own "Solar System."
Make the short strands a little longer and float crystals, a moon charm, and different-sized accent beads for "planets."

Clustered Charms Illusion Necklace

$\mathbb{T}$urn a handful of beads into a pretty cluster of charms that dangles from your necklace. Crystals or **opalescent** beads (see page 35) are the perfect accent beads for the strand.

To make the dangle:

1 Slip one heart onto the head pin and add five seed beads. With the pliers, form a small loop at the end of the pin. Repeat with the other head pin.

*See Techniques, pages 124–130.

2 Attach the 4-mm jump ring* to the lentil bead. Attach the pins and the lentil bead to the larger jump ring.

WHAT YOU NEED
8-mm heart beads (2), different colors
Head pin (2)
Silver or gold seed beads (5)
Needle-nose pliers
4-mm jump ring
Deep blue opalescent lentil bead
7-mm jump ring
20" (50 cm) of 4-lb (1.85-kg) clear monofilament
5- to 7-mm accent beads (2 pairs)
Crimp (10)
Clasp
Jump ring

To make the necklace:

3 Slide the jump ring with the charms to the center of the monofilament.

4 Slide on a crimp, then an accent bead, then a crimp. Decide where you want the bead and then attach the crimps*. Crimp the matching accent bead in place on the other side of the jump ring.

Repeat to attach the remaining accent beads.

5 Attach a crimp to form a loop* in each end of the monofilament. Attach a clasp* to one loop and a jump ring* to the other loop.

Lentil Beads

These small, round, irresistibly smooth disks look just like their namesake — but they come in much more appealing colors! Plus, they have a handy hole in the top so you can dangle them any-where. You can buy them individually or in tubes.

The Savvy Bead Buyer

Flower & Seed Bead Illusion Necklace

*T*his delicate necklace of tiny blue flowers floating around your neck has a sparkling silver bead to highlight the heart of each blossom.

1 Draw two lines on the foam board or paper: 1 1/2" (3.5 cm) and 3/4" (2 cm).

WHAT YOU NEED
Pencil
Piece of foam board or paper
Ruler or measuring tape
20" (50) cm) of 4-lb (1.85-kg) clear monofilament
Flower beads: tiny slightly cupped flowers with a hole in the center (6)
Silver seed beads (6)
Crimp (2)
Needle-nose pliers
Scissors
Clasp
Jump ring

2 Fold the monofilament in half. Slide on one flower bead and, using your line as a reference, position it as shown.

center

3/4" (2 cm)

Slide on a seed bead and pull the thread back through the flower bead so the seed bead sits on top.

3 Working one side and then the other, use your line as a reference to position the remaining five bead pairs, following the pattern shown here:

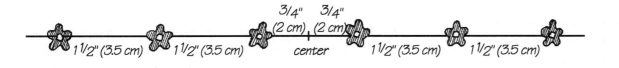

4 Attach a crimp to form a loop* in one end of the monofilament. Looking in the mirror, hold the necklace around your neck and adjust the length to your taste; it looks best lying fairly tightly against your neck. Attach a crimp to form a loop in the other end at that length. Trim the end of the monofilament if necessary. Attach a clasp* to one end of the necklace and a jump ring* to the other end.

Want to Outshine Everyone?

*Check out plastic **miracle beads** from Japan. They're coated with the same reflective paint that makes cars gleam — their super-bright colors are awesome!*

*See Techniques, pages 124–130.

Pearl "Poppers" Illusion Necklace

*How difficult? Moderate
Time: 45 minutes*

The flash of metallic fishing line contrasts elegantly with the gleaming pretend pearls (see page 33) that "pop" out of the center of the necklace. Scoop necklines and tank tops set off this necklace beautifully.

To form the pearl "poppers":

1 Slide one 5-mm pearl to the center of the long piece of fishing line.

WHAT YOU NEED

WHAT YOU NEED
5-mm pretend pearls (3)
16" (40 cm) of plastic-coated copper or silver fishing line
Crimp (16)
Needle-nose pliers
2" (5 cm) of the same fishing line (2)
3-mm pretend pearls (8)
Clasp

2 Attach a crimp* to the end of one of the short pieces of line; slide on two 3-mm pearls and attach another crimp so it's snug against them.

3 Slide the open end of the short beaded line through the larger pearl on the monofilament. Finish the end with crimps and pearls as shown in step 2.

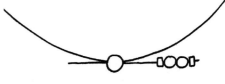

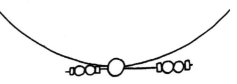

See Techniques, pages 124–130.

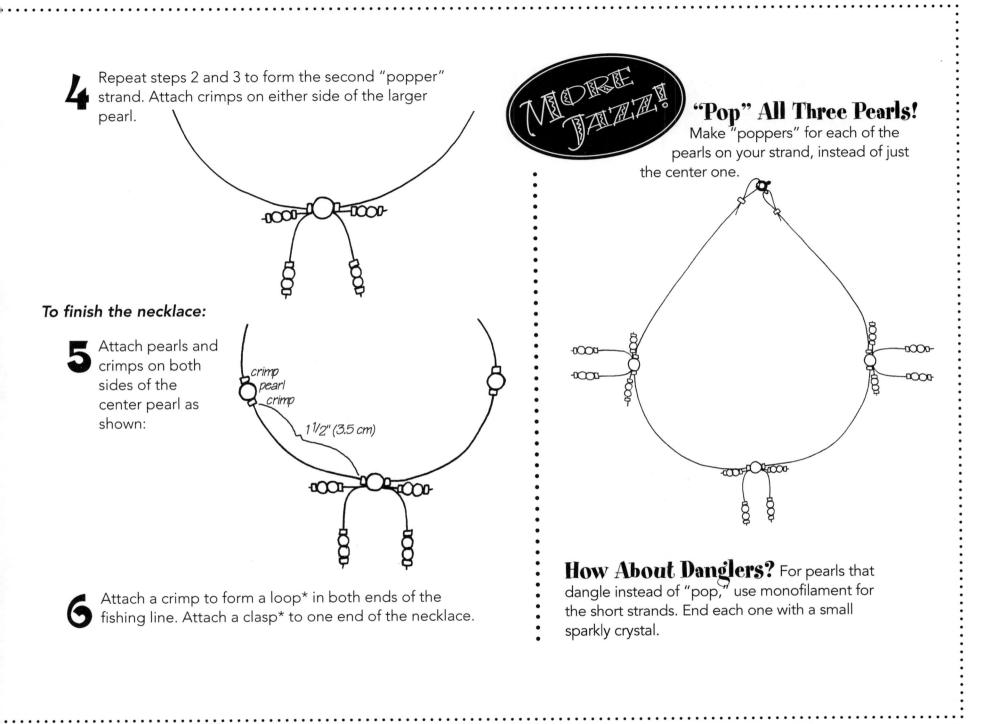

4 Repeat steps 2 and 3 to form the second "popper" strand. Attach crimps on either side of the larger pearl.

To finish the necklace:

5 Attach pearls and crimps on both sides of the center pearl as shown:

crimp
pearl
crimp

1 1/2" (3.5 cm)

6 Attach a crimp to form a loop* in both ends of the fishing line. Attach a clasp* to one end of the necklace.

MORE JAZZ!

"Pop" All Three Pearls!
Make "poppers" for each of the pearls on your strand, instead of just the center one.

How About Danglers? For pearls that dangle instead of "pop," use monofilament for the short strands. End each one with a small sparkly crystal.

Silver & Green Dangles Illusion Necklace

How difficult? Moderate
Time: 1 hour

𝕀*n the mood to look sophisticated? This delicate necklace with its striking combination of silver beads and pale green crystals will do it!*

To make the necklace:

1 Attach a crimp to form a loop* in one end of the monofilament.

2 Slide on eight silver seed beads. Then, slide on crystals, seed beads, and eye pins as shown, finishing with eight silver seed beads:

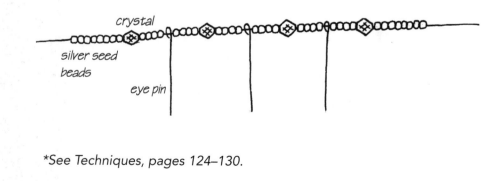

crystal

silver seed beads

eye pin

See Techniques, pages 124–130.

3 Attach a crimp to form a loop in the other end of the monofilament. Attach a clasp* to one end of the necklace and a jump ring* to the other end.

To finish the dangles:

4 Slide the seed beads and crystals onto the eye pins in the pattern shown:

Kink* the eye pin as close as possible to the bottom crystal.

silver seed beads

crystal

WHAT YOU NEED

Crimp (2)
18" (45 cm) of 4-lb (1.85-kg) clear monofilament
Needle-nose pliers
Silver seed beads (64)
2-mm green crystals (10)
Eye pin (3)
Clasp
Scissors
Jump ring

Butterfly Hair Dangle

An open hair pin works perfectly to give the illusion of an elegant gold butterfly alighting on your head. Let the ribbons sway with your hair or dangle them from your ponytail, French braid, or twist for a sophisticated look.

How difficult? Easy!
Time: 10 minutes

1 Slide the butterfly button onto the center of the pin; attach a crimp* on both sides.

2 Center the ribbon on the shank and tie it on with a double knot*.

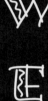

3 Decorate each side of the ribbon with beads as shown in finished dangler, securing each one with a single knot.*

*See Techniques, pages 124–130.

WHAT YOU NEED

Gold-tone butterfly button with a shank (loop) on the back

Large crimp (2)

"Open" hair pin (from drugstore or beauty supply store)

Needle-nose pliers

22" (55 cm) of narrow gold fabric ribbon

4-mm beads (6) , in clear, gold, or in a color to match your outfit

Triple-Strand Illusion Headband

With this headband, nothing has to match if you don't want it to — it's a collection of your favorite beads, scattered wherever you like! Try a combination of glass seed beads and accent beads in colors that will contrast nicely with your hair.

WHAT YOU NEED

24" (60 cm) of thick stretchy clear monofilament (3)

Ruler or measuring tape

Pencil

Size 6 glass beads (70 to 90), in assorted colors and shapes

Accent beads (24 to 36)

Small crimp (21)

Needle-nose pliers

Large crimp (2)

Scissors

Before you start:

You want the scattered beads to lie on the middle 7" to 8" (17.5 to 20 cm) of the strands. Fold each strand in half, and follow the illustration. You'll attach your bead clusters between the crimp and the pencil mark.

Attach a crimp here

Lightly mark string

4" (10 cm)

center

To make each strand:

 Starting in the middle and working from one side to the other, attach a crimp*, slide on two to three glass beads and one to two accent beads, and attach another crimp.

Leave 1" to 2" (2.5 to 5 cm) between the crimps so that the beads can slide around. Continue until you've used all your beads.

To finish the headband:

2 Slide one large crimp over both ends of all three strands (six strands in all). Try the headbands on and adjust them to get the right length. Attach the crimp*.

See Techniques, pages 124–130.

The Inside Scoop
Crimp Won't Fit?

If you have trouble finding a crimp large enough for all three strands, use three large crimps to crimp the ends of each strand separately. Then, wear all three strands together.

DESIGNING ILLUSION JEWELRY: PLAY WITH YOUR BEADS!

This illusion headband is the perfect way to combine odds and ends, like those leftover single beads that you've been saving just because you liked them, as well as to show off interesting accent beads. Mix sizes or keep them all the same. Make your patterns symmetrical or scatter your beads unevenly for a wild effect — remember, you're the designer!

Not sure how to get started? Pin a piece of paper to your foam board and draw a line for each strand of your headband. Pin on different arrangements of beads until you have one you like. Then, tape your monofilament right below the line and transfer the beads, following your pattern.

Swinging Hair Dangle

Swing some beads right along with your long hair or ponytail. Try a mix of stars and hearts — and don't forget a few crystals for some flash!

WHAT YOU NEED

10" (25 cm), 11" (27.5 cm), and 12" (30 cm) of 4-lb (1.85-kg) of clear monofilament
Crimp (12 to 15)
Ruler or measuring tape
Accent beads (12 to 16)
Bright, glittery seed beads and bugle beads (45 to 75)
Tension clip
Needle-nose pliers
Craft glue

1 Attach a crimp* at one end of each monofilament strand. Slide on a shiny star or other accent bead and several seed beads or bugle beads.

2 Attach a crimp 3" to 4" (7.5 to 10 cm) up from the end. Add another accent bead and several seed beads or bugle beads. Follow that pattern to fill the strand.

Repeat for the other two strands.

*See Techniques, pages 124–130.

3 Slide a crimp onto the end of the monofilament. Loop the strand over the outside of the clip and back through the crimp; attach the crimp.

Repeat with the other two strands, spacing them along the clip.

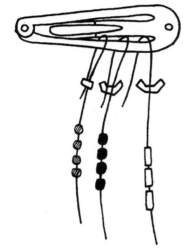

Add a drop of glue at each bottom crimp (to be sure you don't lose the beads) and let it dry.

MORE JAZZ!

Dangle a "Beady" Charm.
Add a ladybug (see page 50) or flower (see page 32) at the top of one of the danglers near the clip.

Magic Hair Sparkler

$\mathbb{S}$ee if your friends can figure out what's holding this swinging sparkler in your hair! Buy the flat jewels in bags of mixed colors so you can make one to match every outfit.

WHAT YOU NEED

8" (20 cm) of beading thread
Beading needle
Crimp (2)
Needle-nose pliers
Ruler or measuring tape
Sparkling, shiny bugle beads (enough to fill a 4"/10 cm strand), assorted colors
Adhesive-backed Velcro strip
1/2" (1 cm) flat, fake jewel, in a color that contrasts with your hair
Pencil or pen
Scissors

1 Thread the needle; attach a crimp* to the other end. String about 2" (5 cm) of beads.

2 Separate the Velcro and place it "hooked" side down. Place the jewel on the strip and trace around it.

Cut out the shape and peel off the backing.

3 "Sandwich" the thread as shown between the adhesive side of the Velcro cutout and the jewel and press firmly.

4 String another 2" (5 cm) of beads. Attach a crimp* on each thread so that the beads are held firmly against the jewel. Trim the end of the thread.

See Techniques, pages 124–130.

Hair Snappers

Now here's the ultimate illusion of jewels afloat in your hair! Velcro is easier to attach (see page 82), but snaps stay put (a better choice for when the dancing gets wild!).

(see page 82)

1 Separate the snaps; lay the tops *prong side down* on the waxed paper (that part is important!) .

2 Being careful to keep the glue off your skin, squeeze a drop onto the flat side of the snap top as shown. Add the decoration on top, press together with tweezers. Let it dry overnight.

3 To wear, close the snap with a lock of hair between the two halves.

Note: You'll need a grown-up's help to use this type of glue; please see page 134 before starting.

please see page 134 before starting.

How difficult? Very easy!
Time: 1 minute per snapper to assemble
(glue needs to cure overnight)

MORE JAZZ!

In Full Bloom! Glue tiny fabric rosebuds or daisies on snaps for a garden in your hair!

WHAT YOU NEED
Large snaps
Waxed paper
Decorative items to attach to your snaps: flat jewels, pearl clusters, large accent beads
Strong glue*
Tweezers

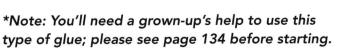

Crystal & Pearl Cluster Illusion Headband

How difficult? Moderate
Time: 1 hour

This circle of real pearls (see page 33) and crystals lies in a magical sparkling arc on your hair!

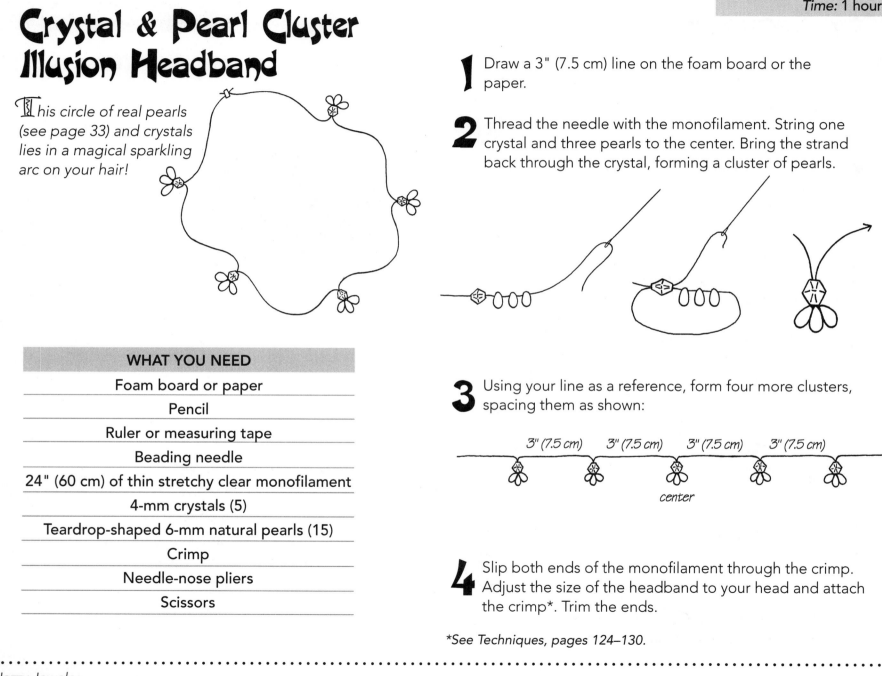

WHAT YOU NEED

Foam board or paper
Pencil
Ruler or measuring tape
Beading needle
24" (60 cm) of thin stretchy clear monofilament
4-mm crystals (5)
Teardrop-shaped 6-mm natural pearls (15)
Crimp
Needle-nose pliers
Scissors

1 Draw a 3" (7.5 cm) line on the foam board or the paper.

2 Thread the needle with the monofilament. String one crystal and three pearls to the center. Bring the strand back through the crystal, forming a cluster of pearls.

3 Using your line as a reference, form four more clusters, spacing them as shown:

3" (7.5 cm)   3" (7.5 cm)   3" (7.5 cm)   3" (7.5 cm)

center

4 Slip both ends of the monofilament through the crimp. Adjust the size of the headband to your head and attach the crimp*. Trim the ends.

See Techniques, pages 124–130.

Tattoo Jewelry

The intricate patterns of tattoo jewelry are one of the coolest styles to come along in years. You can twist and loop strands of tinted monofilament to create tight-fitting necklaces, bracelets, anklets, and rings that look as if they're drawn right on your skin! And the clear version that's so perfect for illusion jewelry (see pages 59–84) will create an intriguing and colorful "tattoo" of beads that magically "float" around your neck, arm or ankle. These patterns may *look* impossible, but once you get the knack of creating the loops, you'll be designing your own tattoos!

THE TATTOO TECHNIQUE: LEARNING TO "LOOP"

To create the tattoo patterns in this chapter, you'll use one or more strands of monofilament (see page 60) or plastic-coated wire (see page 87) to form a series of loops, holding them in place with beads.

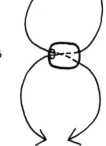

A *crossing bead* holds two crisscrossing strands

A *catching bead* holds a loop when the strands pass through the bead in the same direction

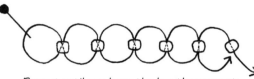

To begin looping:

Fold a long strand of 10-lb (4.5-kg) monofilament in half. Pin or tape it in place.

Now, try this very easy pattern:

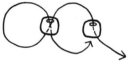

Repeat until you have the length you want.

If you want to jazz it up, use more than one crossing bead OR string beads onto the bottom of the loop.

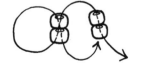

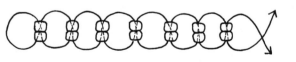

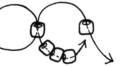

LEARNING TO "LOOP" continued

Once you're comfortable with the one-strand loop, try this double-loop pattern, which starts with two strands side by side.

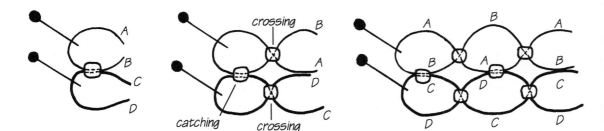

Repeat the pattern as long as you like.

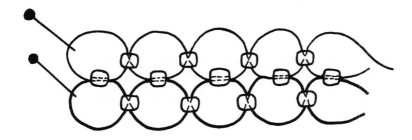

Congratulations! You're ready to roll with any of the jewelry in this chapter!

The Inside Scoop

Plastic or Wire?

Plastic-coated wire is the easiest material to tattoo with, so it's perfect for those first projects where you're still getting used to forming loops and following the pattern. Plus, it creates tighter tattoo jewelry than you can buy; the pieces available in the stores are made with nylon materials, which will stretch out over time.

Monofilament comes in all kinds of colors (even rainbow tones!). The thicker weights are easier to use, so start with at least 10-lb (4.5-kg). You'll have fewer color choices with plastic fishing line but large spools of it are inexpensive.

HOW TO

THE CLASSIC TATTOO

This technique is how the tattoo look began — a doubled strand of tinted monofilament woven into a intricate pattern that's held together only with loops. The looping may take a few tries, but once you get the hang of it, you'll fall into a relaxing rhythm — similar to braiding a friendship bracelet or doing finger knitting!

Double a length of 3' (90 cm) of 10-lb (4.5-kg) monofilament; attach a crimp to form a loop* in the end. Pin the loop to your pillow or your jeans and get settled in a comfortable spot.
Now follow these two steps:

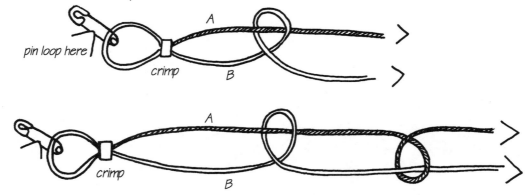

That's all there is to the pattern! If you're having trouble, try repeating "B over A, A over B" as you work.

Be sure to pinch the last loop between your nonlooping fingers until you form the next loop. Don't worry if your loops are uneven at first — you can move them around and reshape them if necessary.

*See Techniques, pages 124–130.

Once you're comfortable with forming the loops, you can add beads of any kind anywhere you want!

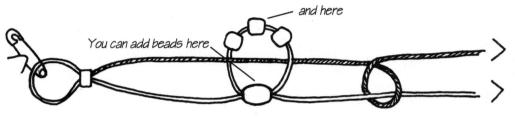

and here

You can add beads here

Stop whenever you reach the length that will go around your neck (or wherever you want to wear it). Then, cut the monofilament and attach a crimp to form a loop* in the end. Attach a clasp to one end.

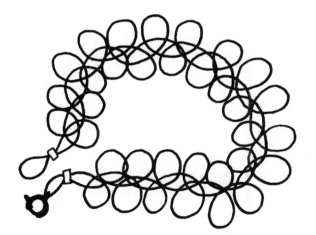

Single-Row Seed Bead Tattoo Bracelet

Easy and delicate, these floating, beaded curves are punctuated by dots of sparkle!

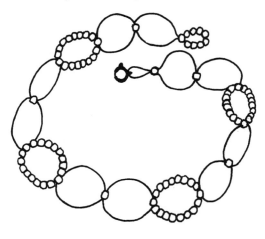

WHAT YOU NEED

Seed beads (about 100)
Ruler or measuring tape
18" (45 cm) of 10- to 12-lb (4.5- to 5.5-kg) monofilament
Foam board or stiff cardboard
Quilting pin or tape
Crimp
Needle-nose pliers
Clasp

1 Slide eight seed beads onto the center of the monofilament. Slide a catching bead (see page 86) over both ends and move it all the way down to form a loop.

Pin the loop to the foam board or tape it to the cardboard.

2 Now, repeat this three-step pattern with crossing beads (see page 86) to make a chain of 3/4" (2 cm) loops:

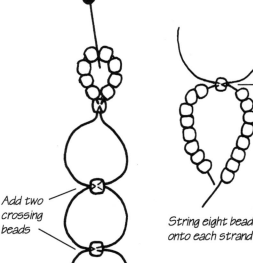

Add two crossing beads

Second crossing bead

String eight beads onto each strand

Add a crossing bead to hold those beads in place

3 When you have eight beaded loops (or whatever number fits your wrist comfortably), attach a crimp to form a loop* on the end of the monofilament. Attach a clasp* to that loop.

MORE JAZZ!

Vary the Bead Pattern:
Add beads only on the bottom of the beaded oval.

Add an accent bead in the middle for your crossing bead, or use two or more crossing beads.

BE A TATTOO DESIGNER!

All of these patterns will work as necklaces, bracelets, or anklets. Just change the final length to make the piece *you* want! What's more, a little variation from the patterns we show here will make the jewelry truly your own super style. So experiment and use your imagination, adding beads to get a look you like or making loops bigger (starting with a longer piece of monofilament) or smaller. Just remember to keep checking the length so that your jewelry is a custom fit for you.

For every tattoo inch (cm), figure on needing 7" (17.5 cm) of strand and 18 seed beads.

*See Techniques, pages 124–130.

Pearl & Steel Double-Loop Tattoo Bracelet

Give your pearls some "attitude" by mixing them with "steel" tattoo loops. Flash them on your wrist or higher up as an armband.

WHAT YOU NEED
18" (45 cm) of plastic-coated metal fishing line (2)
Large crimp (2)
Needle-nose pliers
Quilting pin or tape
Foam board or stiff cardboard
3-mm pretend pearls (about 30)
Ruler or measuring tape
Clasp
Jump ring

1 Holding the wires together, fold them in half and attach a crimp at one end to form a loop*. Pin the loop to the foam board or tape it to the cardboard.

A   B   C   D

*See Techniques, pages 124–130.

2 Repeat this two-step pattern of catching and crossing beads (see page 86) to form a chain of 1/2" (1 cm) loops:

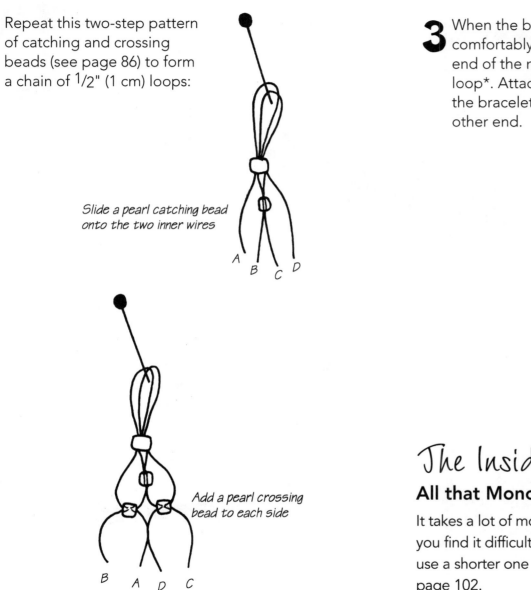

Slide a pearl catching bead onto the two inner wires

A B C D

Add a pearl crossing bead to each side

B A D C

3 When the bracelet fits your wrist comfortably, attach a crimp to the end of the monofilament to form a loop*. Attach a clasp* to one end of the bracelet and a jump ring* to the other end.

The Inside Scoop
All that Monofilament ...

It takes a lot of monofilament to form all those loops! If you find it difficult to work with such a long piece, you can use a shorter one and just keep adding more as shown on page 102.

How difficult? Moderate
Time: 1 1/2 hours

Butterflies & Beads Tattoo Necklace

What's more romantic than butterflies nestling among a shimmer of sparkling silver and frosted blue beads?

WHAT YOU NEED
3' (90 cm) of 10- to 12-lb (4.5- to 5.5-kg) monofilament (2)
Crimp (2)
Quilting pin or tape
Needle-nose pliers
Foam board or stiff cardboard
Size 10 sparkling silver seed beads (53)
Size 6 frosted blue seed beads (19)
Butterfly beads with an up-and-down hole (2)
Clasp
Jump ring

1 Fold the monofilament in half. Attach a crimp to form a loop* in one end. Pin the loop to your foam board or tape it to the cardboard.

See Techniques, pages 124–130.

2 Follow this two-step pattern of catching and crossing beads (see page 86) to form a chain of 1/2"(1 cm) loops:

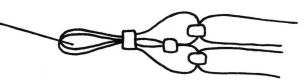

Slide a silver catching bead onto two inner wires

Add a silver crossing bead to each side

Continue until you have five silver catching beads

3 At the sixth catching bead, add blue and butterfly beads to the pattern as shown:

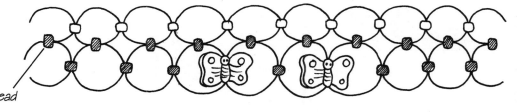

▨ *Blue*

▢ *Silver*

Sixth catching bead

4 Then, return to only silver beads for five more catching beads.

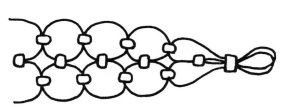

5 Attach a crimp to form a loop in the end. Attach a clasp* to one end of the necklace and a jump ring* to the other end.

The Savvy Bead Buyer

Frosted Beads

*When a bead is **frosted,** it has been tumbled in sand to roughen its exterior. That process softens the finish, giving the bead a dull sheen that reflects the light in an intriguing way.*

Diamond Dazzler Tattoo Necklace

Load the arcs of the loops with seed beads to create an amazing diamond pattern!

WHAT YOU NEED

4' (120 cm) 10- to 12-lb (4.5- to 5.5-kg) monofilament (2), colored or clear

Crimp (2)

Needle-nose pliers

Quilting pin or tape

Foam board or stiff cardboard

Seed beads (about 360), in the color of your choice

Clasp

Scissors

Jump ring

1 Fold both pieces of monofilament in half. Attach a crimp to form a loop* in one end. Pin the loop to your foam board or tape it to the cardboard.

See Techniques, pages 124–130.

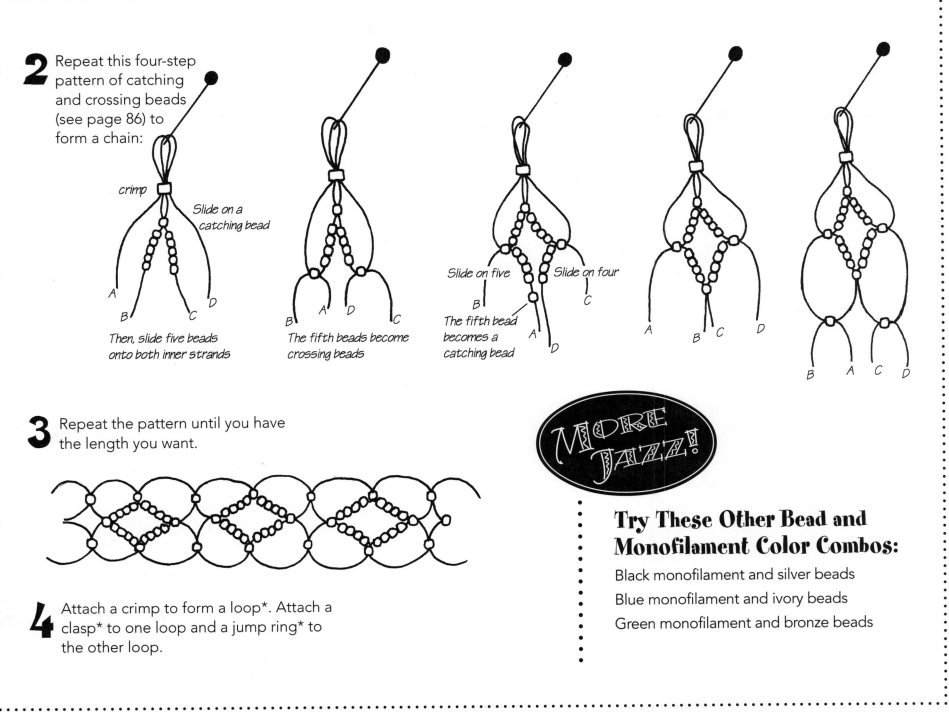

2 Repeat this four-step pattern of catching and crossing beads (see page 86) to form a chain:

crimp

Slide on a catching bead

A   D

B   C

Then, slide five beads onto both inner strands

B   A   D   C

The fifth beads become crossing beads

Slide on five   *Slide on four*

B   C

The fifth bead becomes a catching bead

A   D

A   B   C   D

B   A   C   D

3 Repeat the pattern until you have the length you want.

4 Attach a crimp to form a loop*. Attach a clasp* to one loop and a jump ring* to the other loop.

MORE JAZZ!

Try These Other Bead and Monofilament Color Combos:

Black monofilament and silver beads

Blue monofilament and ivory beads

Green monofilament and bronze beads

Loops & Stars Tattoo Necklace

Catch a neckful of iridescent falling stars with these shining copper loops!

WHAT YOU NEED

18" (45 cm) of plastic-coated copper fishing line (2)
Crimp (2)
Needle-nose pliers
Foam board or stiff cardboard
Quilting pin or tape
Iridescent pale pink star beads (about 21)
Size 11 sparkly silver seed beads (about 42)
Clasp
Scissors, nail clippers, wire cutters
Jump ring

1 Fold the two strands of fishing line in half and attach crimp to form a loop* in one end. Pin the loop to the foam board or tape it to the cardboard.

A   B   C   D

See Techniques, pages 124–130.

Now, follow this three-step pattern of crossing beads (see page 86):

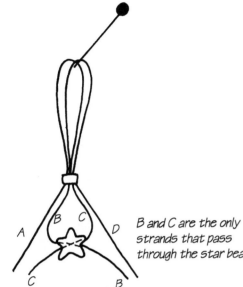

B and C are the only strands that pass through the star beads

String a star crossing bead onto the two inner strands

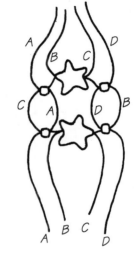

The center strands (B & C) now move from the inside of the one-loop row to the outside of the two-loop row

Add a crossing bead on both sides

The outside strands (A & D) move to the inside of the two-loop row and then out again, but never pass through the star

Add another crossing bead on both sides and then string a star crossing bead on the inner strands

3 Repeat the pattern until you have the right length for your neck.

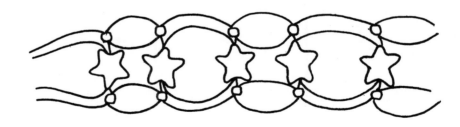

4 Attach a crimp to form a loop*. Attach a clasp* to one loop and a jump ring* to the other loop.

Single-Strand Beaded Tattoo Necklace

This striking and elegant tattoo can go anywhere — your ankle, your wrist, or upper arm!

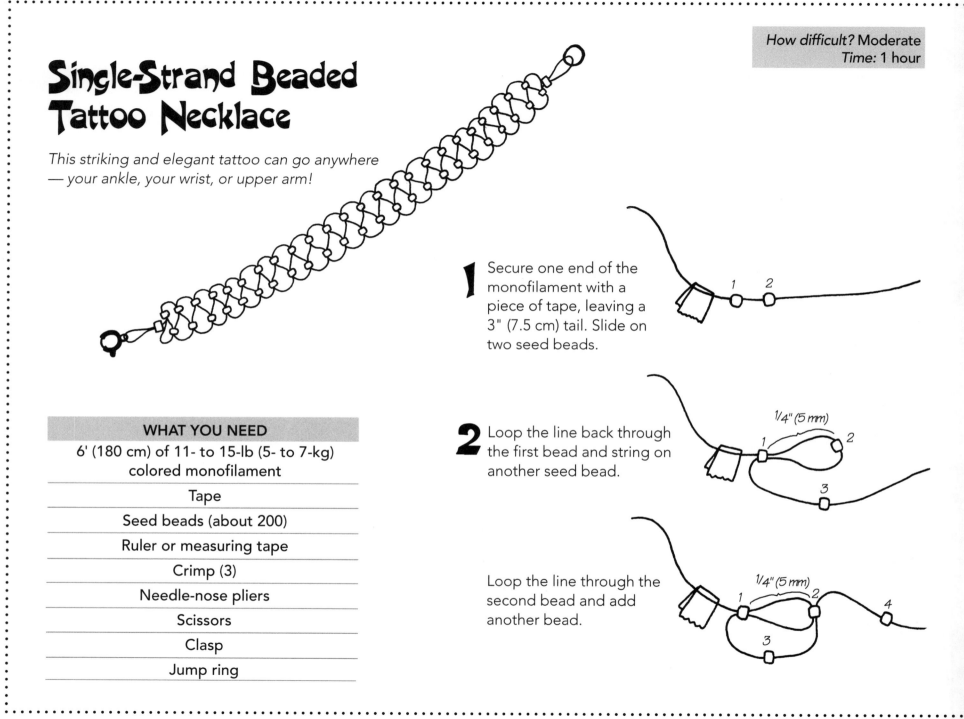

WHAT YOU NEED

6' (180 cm) of 11- to 15-lb (5- to 7-kg) colored monofilament

Tape

Seed beads (about 200)

Ruler or measuring tape

Crimp (3)

Needle-nose pliers

Scissors

Clasp

Jump ring

1 Secure one end of the monofilament with a piece of tape, leaving a 3" (7.5 cm) tail. Slide on two seed beads.

2 Loop the line back through the first bead and string on another seed bead.

1/4" (5 mm)

Loop the line through the second bead and add another bead.

1/4" (5 mm)

Continue, looping through the
prior bead and adding another
bead every time you've entered
a bead a second time.

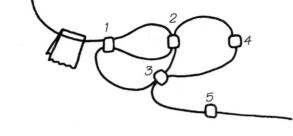

3 Repeat pattern until you reach a comfortable length.

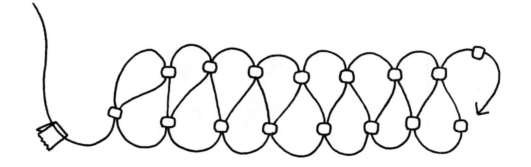

4 Attaach a crimp* just after the last bead.
Finish by attaching a crimp to form a loop* in
each end. Attach a clasp* to one end and a
jump ring* to the other.

*See Techniques, pages 124–130.

OOPS! DIDN'T START WITH ENOUGH MONO?

Cut another generous length of monofilament. Now, follow these steps to work in the new piece:

Near a bead, attach a crimp to hold the old and new pieces of monofilament together.

Loop with both the old and new pieces through two more beads. Then, continue looping with just the new piece.

To finish, thread the "tail" of the new piece of monofilament back through two beads and trim. Trim the old piece.

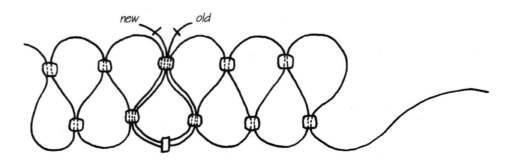

Chokers, Bib Necklaces, Lattice Jewelry, and More!

Whether you like a graceful circle, a swinging fringe, or a sleek, tight-fitting ring of beads, check out these choker styles! Memory wire, a hot new beading "miracle" material, naturally holds a perfect circular choker shape. A dangling fringe (that only *looks* hard to do) will transform that choker into a stylish bib necklace (*and* decorate hair accessories that swing right along with your necklace). And the double-weave technique that gave you all those great "beady" charms (see pages 42–51) is back — this time perfect for weaving a smooth choker (as well as rings!) with just the right fit.

Flower & Seed Bead Choker

This fragile-looking coil is surprisingly easy to make. It clings to your neck for a delicate circle of color.

WHAT YOU NEED

14" (35 cm) of memory wire (see opposite page before cutting)

Needle-nose pliers

Size 11 seed beads (about 200), in the color of your choice

Flower accent beads, 5/16" (8 mm) wide (8), in the same or a contrasting color

Wire cutters

*See Techniques, pages 124–130.

1 Kink* one end of the memory wire.

2 Slide on 30 seed beads.

Add one flower bead, followed by 20 seed beads. Repeat this pattern until you've used all the flower beads.

Finish with 30 seed beads.

3 Kink the other end of the wire.

THANKS FOR THE MEMORIES!

Every once in a while, a new beading supply comes along that launches all kinds of new styles, and memory wire is one of those! This stainless steel flexible wire comes in different-sized coils. When you stretch it out, the metal keeps its "memory" of being a circle, and it springs back into the same-sized coil to wrap around you. It's slender enough that seed beads slide right on — and everything looks good on it!

HOW TO

CUTTING MEMORY WIRE

IMPORTANT! Cutting and bending memory wire takes some strength. You must use real wire cutters, and if you're not careful, it can spring back into its coil and possibly cut you. Please have a grown-up help you with this step, OK?

Beaded Bib Necklace

This fringed choker, with its elegant bib of blue and silver seed and bugle beads, is nothing short of spectacular!

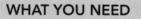

WHAT YOU NEED

Needle-nose pliers

14" (35 cm) of memory wire (see page 105 before cutting)

Size 11 blue seed beads (about 240)

Size 10 silver seed beads (about 20)

24" (60 cm) of beading thread

Beading needle

4-mm silver bugle beads (about 140)

3-mm silver beads (about 20)

Scissors

To make the choker:

1 Kink* one end of the memory wire. Slide on about 6" (15 cm) of blue seed beads, followed by all the size 10 silver seed beads. Finish with the remaining blue seed beads, leaving about 1/4" (5 mm) unfilled.

Kink the end of the wire.

GO ON A FRINGE BINGE!

Bib necklaces, one of the hottest new choker styles, get their jazz from their "bib," a beaded fringe that dangles from the necklace, flashing as it moves. Once you've beaded your choker, you have the perfect "base" for those beaded dangles. (And you can add a fringe to other things too — check out the Fringed Bobby Pin on page 122.) For more on fringing, see page 108.

To make the fringe:

1 Thread one end of the beading needle and tie the other end of the thread to the wire with a lock knot*, leaving 4" (10 cm) of "tail" so you can easily conceal it later.

2 String the beads in this pattern:

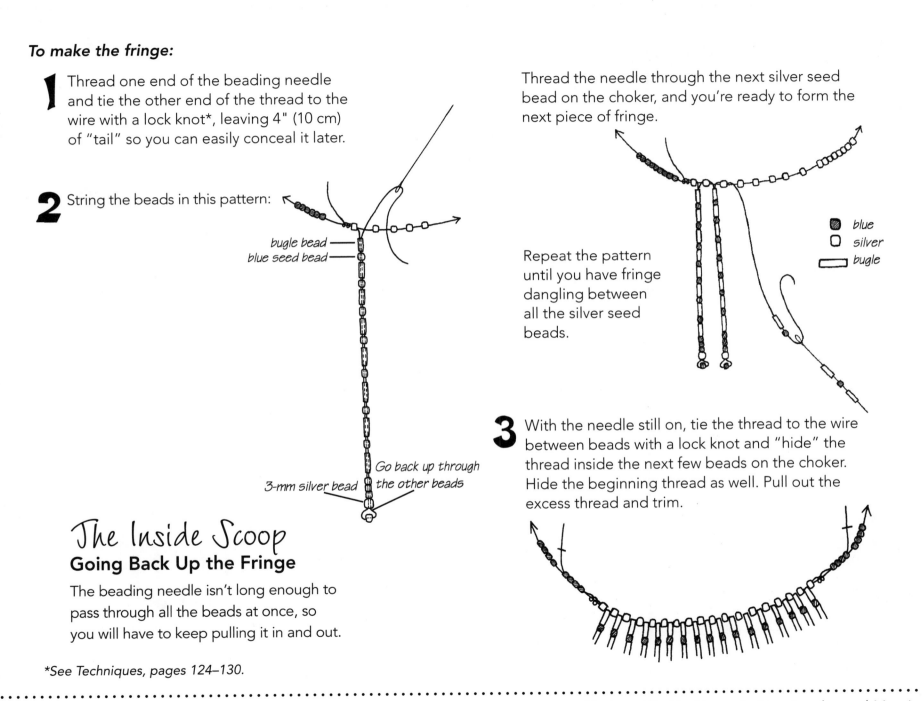

bugle bead

blue seed bead

3-mm silver bead

Go back up through the other beads

Thread the needle through the next silver seed bead on the choker, and you're ready to form the next piece of fringe.

Repeat the pattern until you have fringe dangling between all the silver seed beads.

🔷 blue

⬜ silver

▭ bugle

3 With the needle still on, tie the thread to the wire between beads with a lock knot and "hide" the thread inside the next few beads on the choker. Hide the beginning thread as well. Pull out the excess thread and trim.

The Inside Scoop
Going Back Up the Fringe

The beading needle isn't long enough to pass through all the beads at once, so you will have to keep pulling it in and out.

*See Techniques, pages 124–130.

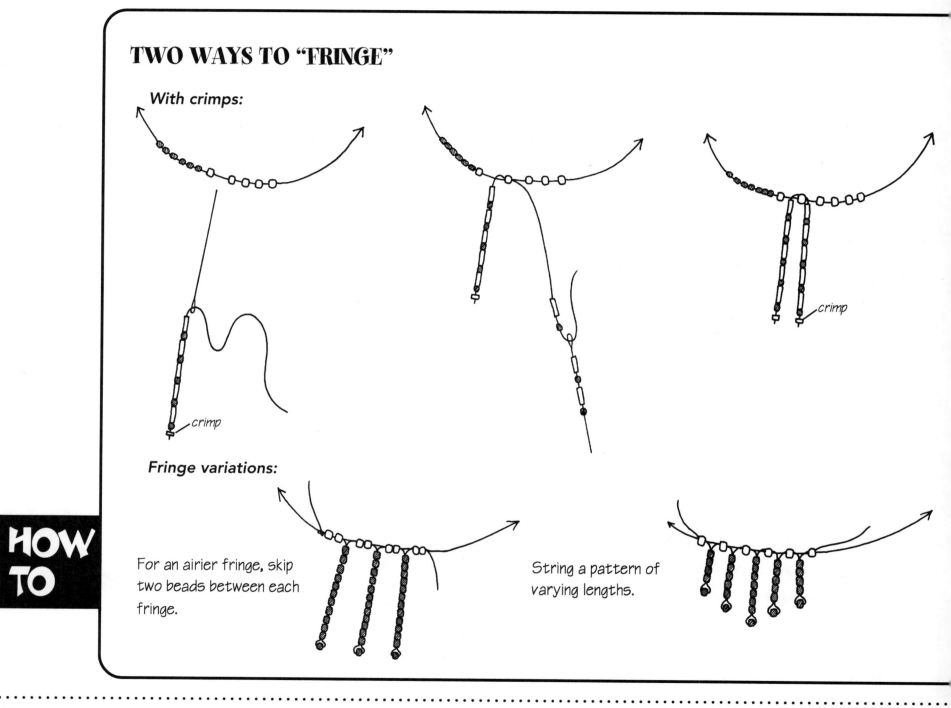

TWO WAYS TO "FRINGE"

With crimps:

crimp

crimp

Fringe variations:

For an airier fringe, skip two beads between each fringe.

String a pattern of varying lengths.

HOW TO

With continuous thread:

If you run out of thread, just follow step 3 of the Beaded Bib Necklace (see page 107). Then, thread a new piece on the needle and tie it to the wire — and you're back in business!

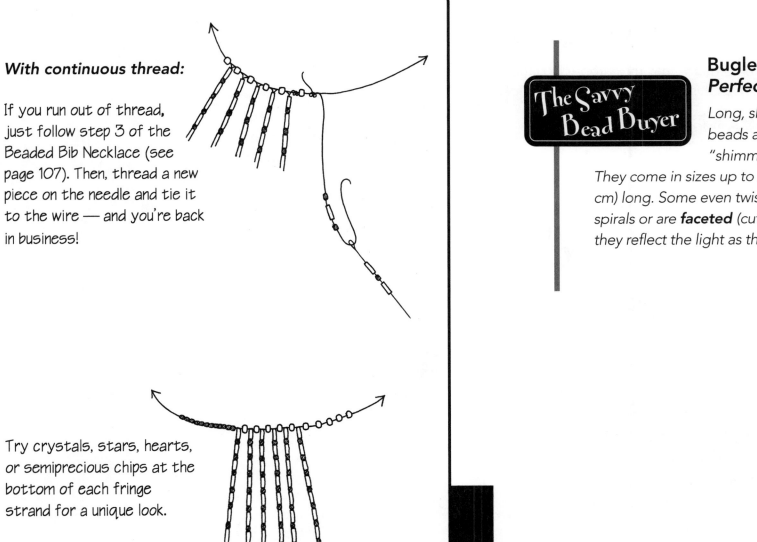

Try crystals, stars, hearts, or semiprecious chips at the bottom of each fringe strand for a unique look.

The Savvy Bead Buyer

Bugle Beads: *Perfect* for Fringes

*Long, slender bugle beads add just the right "shimmy" to your fringe. They come in sizes up to 2" to 3" (5 to 7.5 cm) long. Some even twist into wonderful spirals or are **faceted** (cut on an angle) so they reflect the light as they swing.*

Bugle Bead Lattice Choker

Weave faceted bugle beads into this intriguing pattern (that's so easy to do!) for this sophisticated-looking choker.

How difficult? Easy!
Time: 1 hour

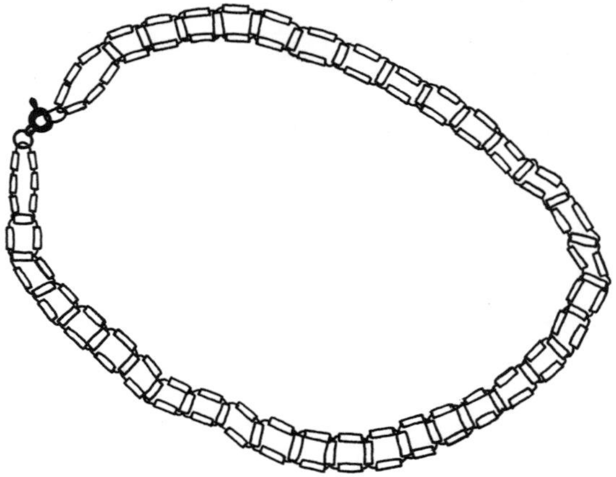

WHAT YOU NEED
Beading needle (2)
3' (90 cm) of beading thread
4-mm gold-faceted bugle beads (about 143)
Quilting pin or tape
Foam board or stiff cardboard
Crimp
Needle-nose pliers
Jump ring (2)
Clasp

1 Thread a needle onto both ends of the thread.

String seven bugle beads and slide them to the middle of the strand.

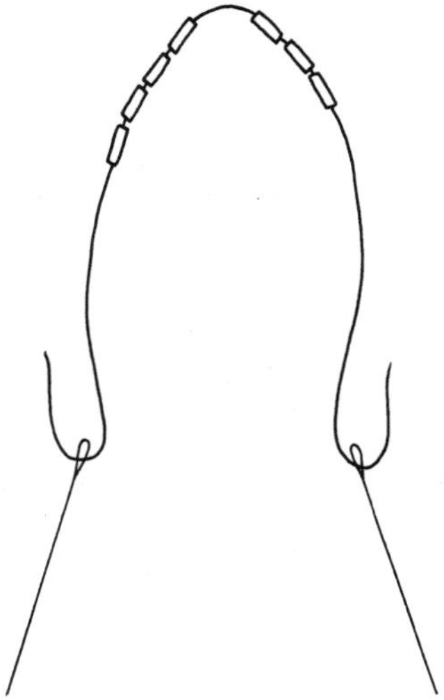

2 Pull one end of the thread through the last bugle bead as shown to form a long loop.

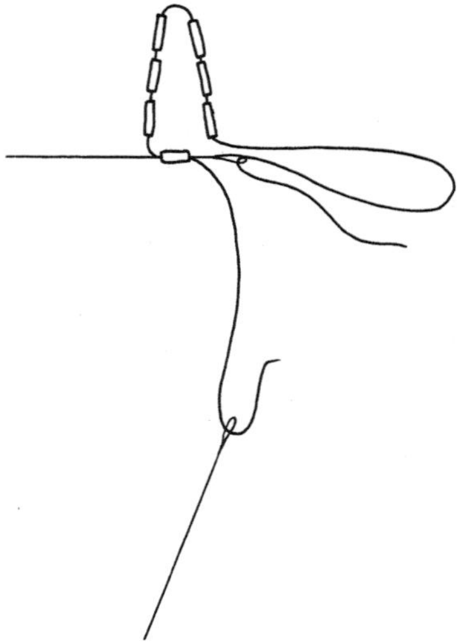

Pin or tape the loop to the foam board or cardboard.

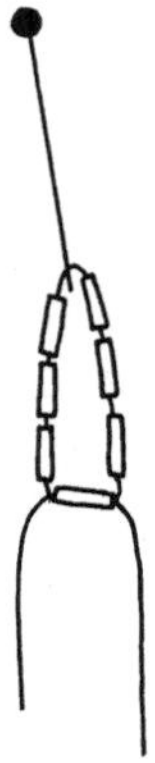

3 String one bugle bead onto one thread end, and two on the other. Pass the end of the one-bead thread through the second bugle bead on the other thread as shown to form the first "square."

String Extra Sparkle! Add a crystal or a pearl between your vertical "crossing" bugle beads.

Continue until you've made 42 squares (or as many as you need to fit your neck comfortably).

4 String three bugle beads onto each thread and tie a lock knot*.

5 Attach a jump ring* to each loop and then attach a clasp* to one end of the necklace.

*See Techniques, pages 124–130.

Seed Bead Lattice Choker with Dangles

This classic choker uses sophisticated iridescent triangle accent beads as dangles.

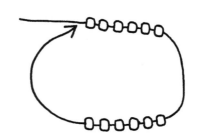

WHAT YOU NEED

Seed beads (about 600 beads for the 6" double-weave section), in the colors of your choice
18" (45 cm) of 28-gauge wire (2)
Ruler or measuring tape
Quilting pin or tape
Foam board or stiff cardboard
3' (90 cm) of beading thread (3)
Beading needle (2)
Teardrop-shaped accent beads (3)
Seed beads for the loops (250)
Jump ring (2)
Clasp
Scissors, nail clippers, or wire cutters

1 Slide six beads to the middle of one piece of wire. Slide six more beads onto one end of the wire.

2 Bring the other end through the second row in a double weave (see Do the Double Weave!, page 44) and pull tight.

3 Continue double-weaving a six-bead-wide row for 1" (2.5 cm), making the beads firm and even. (After a few rows you may find it easiest to pin the work to the foam board or tape it to the cardboard.) Then, bend the wire ends off to the side (you'll finish these later).

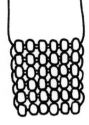

> ## DOUBLE-WEAVING LATTICE JEWELRY
> Double-weaving beads, the technique for making those cute little "beady" charms (see Chapter 2), is also perfect for sleek lattice-style chokers with a perfect fit, because the tightly woven beads lie flat and even. (Need a refresher? See Do the Double Weave!, page 44.)

4 Thread a beading needle onto both ends of one piece of beading thread. Bring it through the first row of beads and center it.

wire

5 Continue double-weaving, six beads per row, for 1" (2.5 cm).

continued next page

6 Now, follow these steps to attach a dangle:

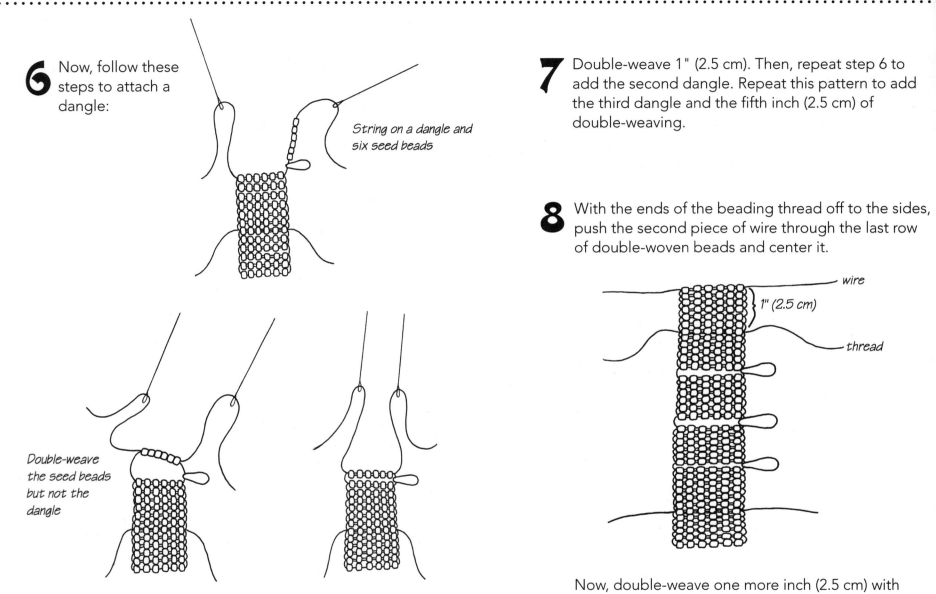

String on a dangle and six seed beads

Double-weave the seed beads but not the dangle

The beads should line up with their row, but the dangle side thread should be loose enough to let the bead fall freely.

7 Double-weave 1" (2.5 cm). Then, repeat step 6 to add the second dangle. Repeat this pattern to add the third dangle and the fifth inch (2.5 cm) of double-weaving.

8 With the ends of the beading thread off to the sides, push the second piece of wire through the last row of double-woven beads and center it.

— wire

1" (2.5 cm)

— thread

Now, double-weave one more inch (2.5 cm) with wire.

To finish the ends:

9 Cut 1' (30 cm) of beading thread; thread a needle onto both ends. Pull it through the last row of the choker strip.

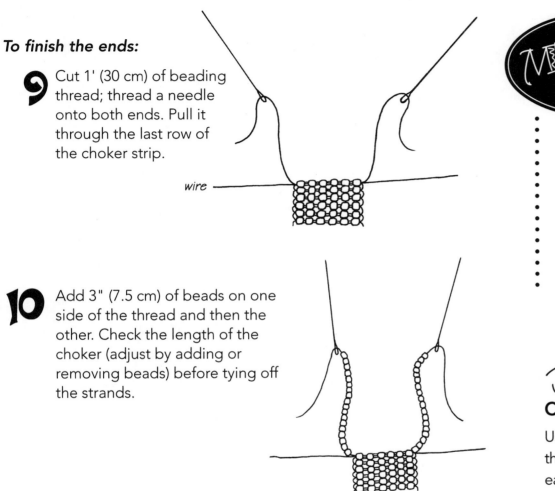

wire

10 Add 3" (7.5 cm) of beads on one side of the thread and then the other. Check the length of the choker (adjust by adding or removing beads) before tying off the strands.

11 Tie the ends in a lock knot*. Attach a jump ring* to one side and a clasp* to the other.

To finish the ends of the beading thread and wire, see page 45.

See Techniques, pages 124–130.

Dazzling Danglers! Try hanging tiny crystals, tinted beads that exactly match your favorite dress (or your eyes!), glittery glass stars, or special charms.

The Inside Scoop
Combining Wire and Thread

Using wire is the easiest way to double weave; the ends are stiff and fine beading wire passes easily through even small bead holes. But an entire choker made with wire can be a little stiff. A double-weave strip made with beading thread, however, is soft and comfortable to wear. This necklace combines these materials for a choker that's both fluid and firm.

Pearl Lattice Ring

*E*legant **pretend pearls** *(see page 33) make a sophisticated, slinky circle for your finger.*

How difficult? Moderate
Time: 45 minutes

1 Thread a needle onto both ends of the elastic thread.

String three pearls to the middle of the thread.

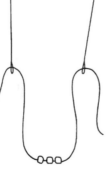

WHAT YOU NEED
18" (45 cm) of elastic thread
Beading needle (2)
3-mm pretend pearls (about 72)
Scissors

2 String three pearls onto the thread and double-weave (See Do the Double Weave!, page 44) them.

Continue to double-weave, three pearls at a time.

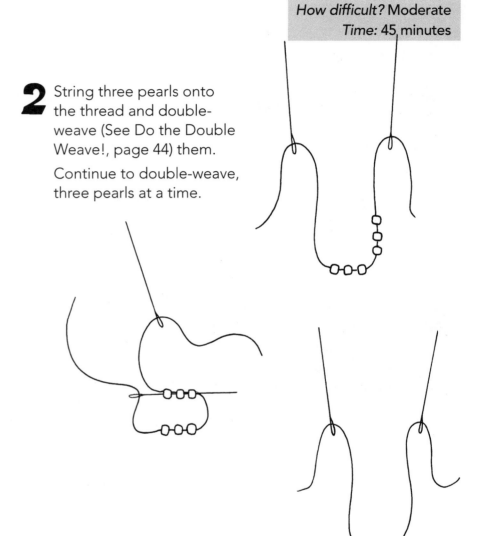

3 When you have a strip that fits snugly around your finger, finish and trim the ends (see page 45).

The Inside Scoop
Working with Two Needles

Elastic thread is perfect for a ring, because you end up with a loop that slips on easily and holds tight. The drawback is that you need two needles, and keeping them both threaded can get a bit cumbersome. The easiest way to work is to pin or tape the jewelry flat on a section of foam board or cardboard.

Keep on Weaving ... and turn this into a stylish pearl cuff. You can make it as wide or as narrow as you like just by varying the number of pearls that make up each row.

LATTICE RINGS: FUN AND FUNKY!

Not in the mood to double-weave an entire choker? Or maybe you don't have enough beads to go around your neck, but you love that particular color and still want to make something. How about a ring?

Lattice rings are small enough to double-weave (see page 44) right in your lap, so they're a great way to pass the time on long car trips.

If size 11 seed beads are a challenge for you to handle comfortably, especially for such a small piece of jewelry, use a larger size, maybe 8 or 6.

Bugle Bead & Seed Bead Lattice Ring

Long shiny bugle beads with a sparkling seed bead on each side make an eye-catching ring.

2 Slide on a seed bead, bugle bead, and seed bead and double-weave (see Do the Double Weave!, page 44) them in place.

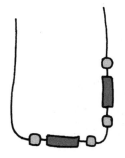

1 Slide on one seed bead, one bugle bead, and another seed bead to the middle of the wire.

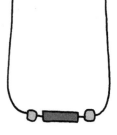

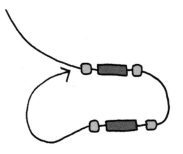

WHAT YOU NEED
Seed beads (about 54)
4-mm bugle beads (about 27)
18" (45 cm) of 34-gauge beading wire
Scissors, nail clippers, or wire cutters
Needle-nose pliers or tweezers

Continue to double-weave in this pattern:

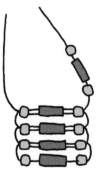

3 When you have a strip that fits snugly around your finger, finish and trim the ends (see page 45).

The Inside Scoop
A Good Fit

Beading wire isn't stretchy like elastic, so you need to be more careful with sizing. Try on your ring frequently while you work.

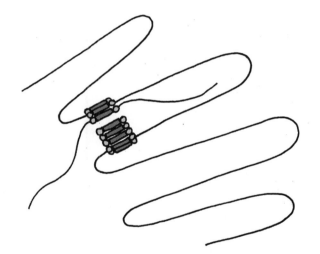

Accent Bead Lattice Ring

A double line of sparkling crystals adds a touch of elegance to this shimmering seed bead ring.

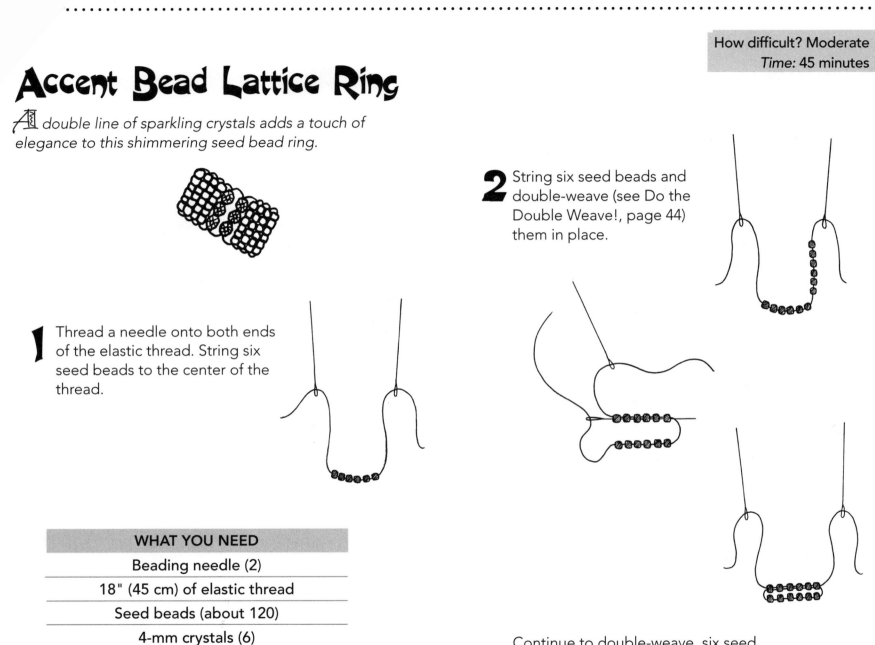

1 Thread a needle onto both ends of the elastic thread. String six seed beads to the center of the thread.

2 String six seed beads and double-weave (see Do the Double Weave!, page 44) them in place.

Continue to double-weave, six seed beads at a time, until you have 10 rows.

WHAT YOU NEED
Beading needle (2)
18" (45 cm) of elastic thread
Seed beads (about 120)
4-mm crystals (6)
Scissors

How difficult? Moderate
Time: 45 minutes

3 Now, double-weave the rows of crystals, three to a row:

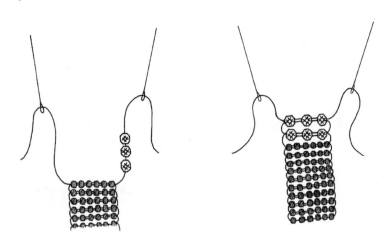

4 Double-weave another 10 rows of seed beads. Check the fit of the ring as you work the final rows, adding or cutting back rows as needed.

5 When you have a strip that fits snugly around your finger, trim and finish the ends (see page 45).

The Inside Scoop
Sort Your Beads

Occasionally you'll find a misshapen seed bead in the batch. Don't use it for double weaving — you'll get an uneven result. Uniform, even beads with nice wide holes will give you a smooth, close-fitting piece of lattice jewelry.

Fringed Bobby Pin

This fringe falls at whatever angle the bobby pin rests in your hair, so use it to pull back your bangs or to hold the wisps around your ponytail or French braid.

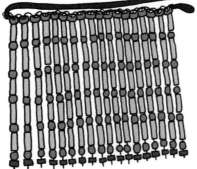

WHAT YOU NEED

18" (45 cm) of 34-gauge beading wire
Bobby pin
Chopstick or pencil
Size 11 green iridescent seed beads (about 96)
Beading needle
24" (60 cm) of beading thread
Crimp (about 16)
Needle-nose pliers
Silver bugle beads (about 90)
Craft glue
Scissors, nail clippers, or wire cutters

To bead the bobby pin:

1 Wrap one end of the 18" (45 cm) section of beading wire around one end of the bobby pin so it's firmly attached.

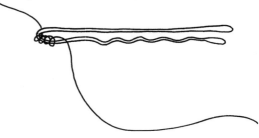

2 Wedge the pin open with the chopstick or pencil to hold it while you work. Slide on one seed bead, and wrap the wire around the pin.

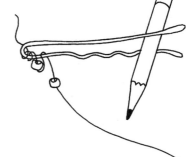

Continue wrapping and beading until you've covered the top of the pin.

3 Wrap the wire around the pin several times and pull it through the coil to be sure everything is nice and tight. Trim the ends.

To make the fringe:

1 Thread the needle with the 24" (60 cm) of beading thread; attach a crimp* to the other end.

2 Using the crimp method (see page 108), add beads in this pattern to make two fringes at a time:

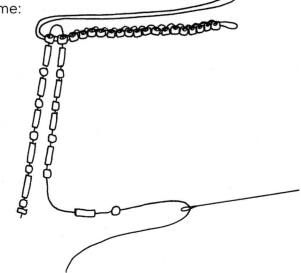

See Techniques, pages 124–130.

3 Repeat steps 1 and 2 until you have filled the pin with fringe.

4 Add a drop of glue to the crimp at the bottom of each fringe and let dry.

The Inside Scoop
Why Use Crimps?

You could work this fringe with the continuous thread technique (see page 109), but crimps are faster. Just be sure to press them tightly shut!

Techniques

Here's a collection of handy how-to for jewelry makers, from knots and loops to crimps and clasps.

Tying Knots

A Single Knot

1. Left over right and through the loop.

2. Pull tight.

A Double Knot

1. Tie a single knot.

2. Now, go right over left and through the loop.

3. Pull tight.

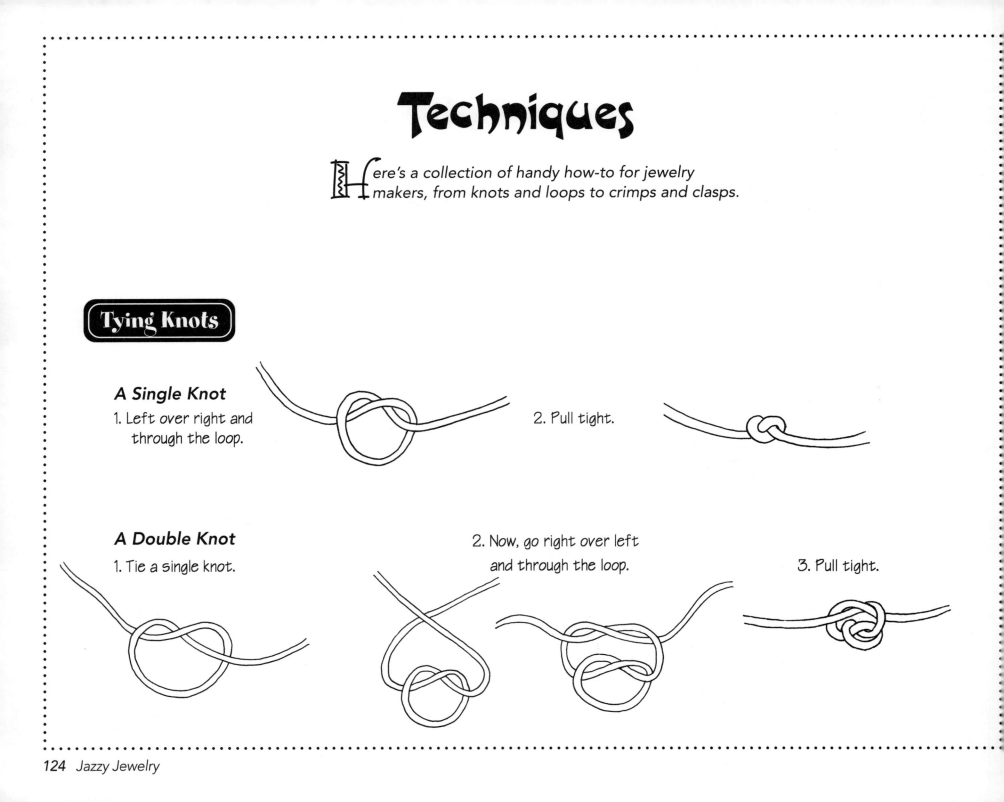

A Lock Knot

A **lock knot** won't slip, whether you're tying elastic, thread, or monofilament.

Tying a lock knot with two ends:

1. Tie a single knot (see page 124).

2. Bring the right end over and through the loop again.

3. Now, go right over left and through the loop.

4. Pull tight.

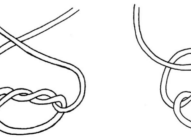
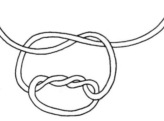
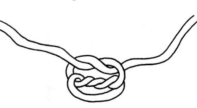

Tying a lock knot onto a loop:

Follow the steps shown above, using the loose end to go over or under the loop.

Forming a Kink

Kinking the End of a Wire Strand

Use your needle-nose pliers to form a tiny loop to hold on your beads.

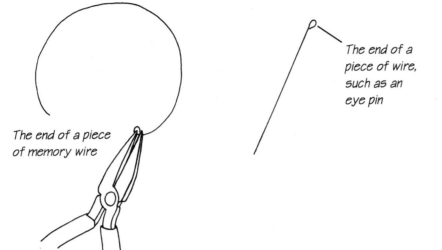

The end of a piece of memory wire

The end of a piece of wire, such as an eye pin

Forming the loop as close as possible to the beads to finish the other end of a memory-wire choker may take some practice. Trim the wire as needed. If you're left with a sharp edge, just glue a bead over the end.

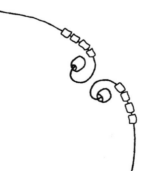

Attaching a Crimp

To position a bead:

Slide the crimp over the strand material to the place where you want it.

With needle-nose pliers, press the crimp shut, being careful not to cut through your strand.

To secure beads at the end of your strand material:

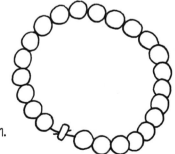

To secure the ends of a strand:

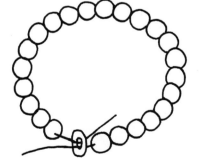

Slide the ends through the crimp from opposite sides.

Close the crimp. If necessary, trim the ends so they're even.

Attaching a Crimp to Form a Loop

Slide the strand (or strands) through the crimp and then back through again to form a loop.

A loop at the end of a necklace or bracelet:

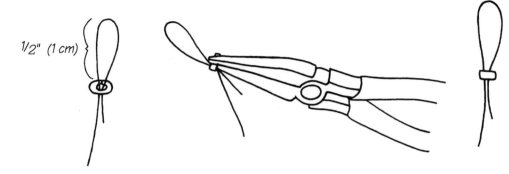

1/2" (1 cm)

A one-strand loop at the beginning of a tattoo necklace:

A two-strand loop:

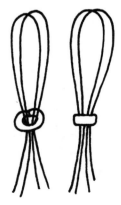

Jump Rings

Attaching a Jump Ring

Using needle-nose pliers, open a jump ring by twisting it like this:

Don't pull it open like this:

Use the pliers to close the jump ring. Make sure the gap is *tightly* closed, especially if you're using very thin monofilament as your strand material.

Attach a jump ring to the loop at the end of a necklace or bracelet that will go opposite the clasp:

or to attach a charm so it dangles:

Attaching a jump ring to the end of a "beady" bracelet:

Wrap the remaining wire ends around a jump ring.

Tuck the ends back through the strand of beads.

Wrap the wires between two beads and trim.

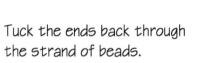

Both of these clasps are easy to attach; you can use either one.

To attach a spring ring:

Using needle-nose pliers, twist open the loop on the spring ring and slip on the loop at the end of your piece of jewelry.

Twist the metal loop tightly shut.

If the loop on the spring ring is a solid piece, attach a jump ring (see page 129) to it first.

To attach a barrel clasp:

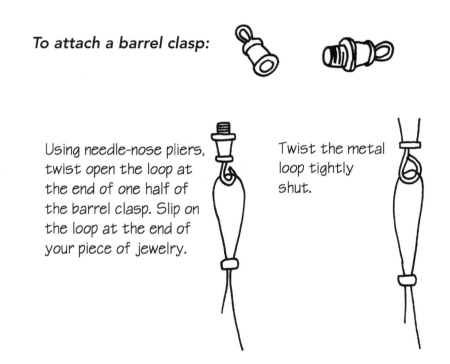

Using needle-nose pliers, twist open the loop at the end of one half of the barrel clasp. Slip on the loop at the end of your piece of jewelry.

Twist the metal loop tightly shut.

Repeat at the other end of the piece of jewelry with the other half of the barrel clasp.

If the loop on the end of the barrel clasp is a solid piece, attach a jump ring (see page 129) to it first.

"Must-Have" Supplies for Jewelry Makers

One of the best things about making jewelry is that you don't need a lot of fancy tools and supplies. After all, all it takes to whip up an armload of bead bracelets is a handful of beads and something to string them on! But as you get hooked on jewelry making — and you will, trust me! — you'll quickly move on to more challenging pieces.

Here's a rundown of the basics so that you'll know exactly what you're looking for in the store.

Beads, Beads, Beads: The Best Part of Jewelry Making!

A bead is just about anything with a hole in it, and I can guarantee that you will never run out of beads to love. They come in an infinite variety of shapes, colors, materials, and sizes, from sparkly crystals and lustrous pearls, to shiny circles and tubes, to colorful flowers, butterflies, stars — you name it!

Beads We Use a Lot of in This Book:

Accent Beads and Charms

These are special decorations that you use carefully here and there for effect, rather than stringing an entire strand with them. You'll find them in a *wide* range of materials: glass, metal, plastic, wood, semiprecious stone, clay, even tiny coils of colored wire.

They're sold individually from little open bins in craft and bead shops, on small strands, or a few to a package.

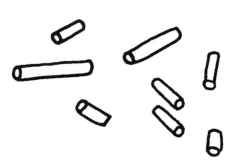

Bugle Beads

Bugle beads are slender tubes of different lengths. Bugle beads have numbered sizes: the *longer* the bead, the *higher* the number.

Beads!

Beads!

Seed Beads

Small, donut-shaped spheres that resemble tiny seeds, these are the basic glass beads sold on strands, in tubes or in small plastic bags.

The numbers indicate the size: the *higher* the number, the *smaller* the bead. Size 11's are the most common.

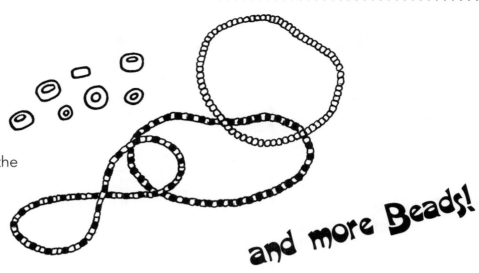

and more Beads!

Making Your Own Beads

Clays like Sculpey and Fimo are great for making your own beads and charms. (They're not really clay. When they're heated, the particles fuse together into a hard plastic.)

Important: *Follow the instructions for using these plastic clays. Always wash your hands after using them. While they're baking, their fumes are very toxic.*

Hot on the Trail of Old Beads

Sometimes there are beads that nobody loves anymore — until you come along! You'll find them on jewelry at thrift shops, flea markets, garage sales, in your mom's and aunts' drawers, attics and basements, even in your own jewelry box. These beads are ripe for cutting and restringing. Just be sure to ask first, so you don't cut up any jewelry that has special memories.

Bead Sizes

Even though beads from different countries will be labeled with the same number, they may be enough of a different size that they won't work with your other beads. Use your eyes to make a good comparison.

Handy Tools and Supplies

Your family probably already has most of the tools you'll need, and if not, none are expensive to buy.

Beading Needles

These long pieces of hair-thin wire are very flexible. Look for ones that have a large eye at the end so you can thread them easily (the eye will flatten to go through the littlest seed bead).

Wire needles don't last; they twist out of shape, so buy them by the pack and expect to go through a lot.

Foam Board

A sheet of foam board, cut down to a comfortable size, makes a great work surface: You can stick quilting pins into it to hold your jewelry steady as you work, as well as mark the board for spacing beads evenly.

Plus, if you have to put your project away for a while, the pins will hold your "work-in-progess" in place.

Quilting Pins

These sewing pins (also called ball-point pins), have large heads, so it's easy to push and pull them in and out of your foam board.

Glue

Occasionally, you'll need a little glue. Usually, it's just a drop to secure something — white craft glue will be fine. Some glues decay plastic, though (which includes monofilament), so check the label.

A few projects in this book require a strong glue as noted. But the better a glue sticks, the more toxic it seems to be. When you use any glue that is not labeled "nontoxic," please ask a grown-up for help. It's very important to keep it off your skin and to avoid breathing it.

Measuring Tape

Use it to measure your neck, wrist, and jewelry for a good fit.

Needle-Nose Pliers

Choose one that fits comfortably in your hand and look for the pointiest "nose" you can find.

Scissors or Nail Clippers

You can use either of these to cut most beading wire, but if you use them frequently, the blades will be ruined for cutting anything else. A sturdy pair of inexpensive kid's scissors is perfect.

Tweezers

Use them for picking up little things (like tiny beads) your fingers can't and for pressing wires tightly together.

Wire Cutters

You'll need a pair of these to cut memory wire (see page 105).

Storing Your Supplies

So you can always find what you need, keep your supplies and tools in little containers labeled "Findings," "Stringing Supplies," "Tools," etc. I like small, inexpensive plastic buckets from home supply stores; I can easily see what's inside, and they stack to fit on shelves. Recycled yogurt cartons, plastic food storage containers, and baskets will also do the job. Little glass bottles or jars and inexpensive plastic tackle boxes make great bead holders.

If you're careful with your tools, they'll last forever. I still have the needle-nose pliers I bought when I was 12 years old. When I'm finished, they go back in my bright red easy-to-find toolbox that I've loved for years.

Findings

indings are all the little "nuts and bolts" that you use to hold your jewelry together. Take a quick look through your jewelry box — you already have most of these pieces on your existing jewelry; you just may not have known what they were called.

Clasps: You can use either of these styles anytime a clasp is called for in this book.

Spring ring

Barrel clasp

Crimp: This soft metal circle is first strung and then pressed flat with needle-nose pliers. Crimps are used to close loops of monofilament or wire (where knots wouldn't hold very well) and to hold beads in place.

Ear Nut: Slides onto the back of the ear post.

Ear Post: The thin metal rod that goes through your pierced ear, with a flat end to hold a decoration.

Ear Wire: The thin metal wire that goes through your pierced ear to hold a dangling earring. There are two types:

Eye Pin: A straight pin that ends in a metal loop. These are great for dangling beads from an ear wire or necklace You kink (see page 126) th other end or attach a crimp (see page 127) to hold the beads on.

Head Pin: A long straight pin with a blunt end. The head keeps beads on, and you kink (see page 126) the other end so you can dangle the pin.

Jump Ring: A little circle of metal to attach a charm or a clasp.

Pronged Rhinestone Back: This flat disk (measured in millimeters) holds a flat-backed rhinestone onto a strand of beads.

Stringing Materials

BEADING THREAD: It pays to go for the good-quality stuff: It's durable and it won't fray. The last thing you want is for your strand to break!

BEADING WIRE: A strong but flexible wire. The thickness is called the "gauge:" the *higher* the number, the *thinner* the wire.

ELASTIC THREAD: Stretchy sewing thread, available in different thicknesses.

MEMORY WIRE: A very stiff sharp wire sold in a coil that holds its circular shape after you bead it. You'll need wire cutters to cut it (see page 105).

MONOFILAMENT: "Mono" is a strong, flexible nylon strand material used for bead stringing, illusion jewelry, and tattoo jewelry. It's also called "illusion cord."

Regular monofilament is sold in different sizes by weight: the *higher* the number of pounds, the *stronger* the stuff.

The stretchy version (sometimes sold as "clear stretchy string,") comes in "thick" and "thin."

Safety Check!

If your household has small children, please don't leave your beading supplies and tools within their reach. This includes dropped beads — they might choke on them.

Be careful with your needles, especially near your eyes. Avoid letting needles roll onto the floor or into chairs — they're very hard to find.

Index

More Good Books from Williamson Publishing

Williamson books are available from your bookseller or directly from Williamson Publishing. Please see last page for ordering information or to visit our website. Thank you.

The original Williamson's *Kids Can!® Books …*

WHERE ALL KIDS CAN SOAR!

The following *Kids Can!®* books for ages 5 to 13 are each 144 to178 pages, fully illustrated, trade paper, 11 x 8 1/2, $12.95 US.

ART & CRAFTS & COOKING

JAZZY JEWELRY
Power Beads, Crystals, Chokers, & Illusion and Tattoo Styles
by Diane Baker

American Bookseller Pick of the Lists
Dr. Toy Best Vacation Product
KIDS' CRAZY ART CONCOCTIONS
50 Mysterious Mixtures for Art & Craft Fun
by Jill Frankel Hauser

Parents' Choice Gold Award
American Bookseller Pick of the Lists
Oppenheim Toy Portfolio Best Book Award
THE KIDS' MULTICULTURAL ART BOOK
Art & Craft Experiences from Around the World
by Alexandra M. Terzian

Parents' Choice Recommended
KIDS' ART WORKS!
Creating with Color, Design, Texture & More
by Sandi Henry

Teachers' Choice Award
Parent's Guide Children's Media Award
Dr. Toy Best Vacation Product
CUT-PAPER PLAY!
Dazzling Creations from Construction Paper
by Sandi Henry

Parents' Choice Approved
Parent's Guide Children's Media Award
MAKING COOL CRAFTS & AWESOME ART!
A Kids' Treasure Trove of Fabulous Fun
by Roberta Gould

American Bookseller Pick of the Lists
Parents' Choice Recommended
ADVENTURES IN ART
Arts & Crafts Experiences for 8- to 13-Year Olds
by Susan Milord

Parents' Choice Approved
KIDS CREATE!
Art & Craft Experiences for 3- to 9-Year-Olds
by Laurie Carlson

American Bookseller Pick of the Lists
Oppenheim Toy Portfolio Best Book Award
Skipping Stones Nature & Ecology Honor Award
EcoArt!
Earth-Friendly Art & Craft Experiences for 3- to 9-Year-Olds
by Laurie Carlson

Parent's Guide Children's Media Award
Benjamin Franklin Best Education/Teaching Book Award
HAND-PRINT ANIMAL ART
by Carolyn Carreiro
full color

Early Childhood News Directors' Choice Award
Real Life Award
VROOM! VROOM!
Making 'dozers, 'copters, trucks & more
by Judy Press

Selection of Book-of-the-Month; Scholastic Book Clubs
KIDS COOK!
Fabulous Food for the Whole Family
by Sarah Williamson & Zachary Williamson

Benjamin Franklin Best Multicultural Book Award
Parents' Choice Approved
Skipping Stones Multicultural Honor Award
THE KIDS' MULTICULTURAL COOKBOOK
Food & Fun Around the World
by Deanna F. Cook

Williamson's
Kaleidoscope Kids® Books ...

WHERE LEARNING MEETS LIFE

Kaleidoscope Kids® books allow children, ages 7 to13, to explore a subject from many different angles, using many different skills. All books are 96 pages, two-color, fully illustrated, 10 x 10, $10.95 US.

WHO <u>REALLY</u> DISCOVERED AMERICA?
Unraveling the Mystery & Solving the Puzzle
by Avery Hart & Paul Mantell

American Bookseller Pick of the Lists
Children's Book Council Notable Book
Dr. Toy 10 Best Educational Products
PYRAMIDS!
50 Hands-On Activities to Experience Ancient Egypt
by Avery Hart & Paul Mantell

American Bookseller Pick of the Lists
Children's Book Council Notable Book
Dr. Toy 100 Best Children's Products
KNIGHTS & CASTLES
50 Hands-On Activities to Experience the Middle Ages
by Avery Hart & Paul Mantell

American Bookseller Pick of the Lists
Parent's Guide Children's Media Award
ANCIENT GREECE!
40 Hands-On Activities to Experience This Wondrous Age
by Avery Hart & Paul Mantell

American Bookseller Pick of the Lists
¡MEXICO!
40 Activities to Experience Mexico Past and Present
by Susan Milord

GOING WEST!
Journey on a Wagon Train to Settle a Frontier Town
by Carol A. Johmann and Elizabeth J. Rieth

Parents' Choice Recommended
BRIDGES!
Amazing Structures to Design, Build & Test
by Carol A. Johmann and Elizabeth J. Rieth

Teachers' Choice Award
GEOLOGY ROCKS!
50 Hands-On Activities to Explore the Earth
by Cindy Blobaum

THE BEAST IN YOU!
Activities & Questions to Explore Evolution
by Marc McCutcheon

Williamson's
Quick Starts for Kids!™ Books

KIDS START SIMPLE — AND GROW THEIR SKILLS!

The following *Quick Starts for Kids!*™ books for ages 8 and older are each 64 pages, fully illustrated, trade paper, 8 x 10, $7.95 US.

BAKE THE BEST-EVER COOKIES!
By Sarah A. Williamson

BE A CLOWN!
Techniques from a Real Clown
by Ron Burgess

MAKE YOUR OWN BIRDHOUSES & FEEDERS
by Robyn Haus

YO–YO!
Tips & Tricks from a Pro!
by Ron Burgess

DRAW YOUR OWN CARTOONS!
by Don Mayne

KIDS' EASY KNITTING PROJECTS
by Peg Blanchette

KIDS' EASY QUILTING PROJECTS
by Terri Thibault

MAKE YOUR OWN BEARS & BEAR CLOTHES
by Sue Mahren

Visit Our Website!

To see what's new at Williamson, learn about our other *Kids Can!*® books, our *Little Hands*® books for 2- to 6-year-olds, and learn more about specific books, visit our website at:

www.williamsonbooks.com

To Order Books:

You'll find Williamson books wherever high-quality children's books are sold, or order directly from Williamson Publishing. We accept Visa and MasterCard *(please include the number and expiration date)*.

**Toll-free phone orders with credit cards:
1-800-234-8791**

Or, send a check with your order to:

**Williamson Publishing Company
P.O. Box 185
Charlotte, Vermont 05445**

E-mail orders with credit cards: **order@williamsonbooks.com**
Catalog request: **mail, phone, or e-mail**

Please add **$4.00** for postage for one book plus **$1.00** for each additional book. Satisfaction is guaranteed or full refund without questions or quibbles.

Prices may be slightly higher when purchased in Canada.

Kids Can!®, *Little Hands*®, *Kaleidoscope Kids*®, and *Tales Alive!*® are registered trademarks of Williamson Publishing.

Good Times™ and *Quick Starts for Kids!*™ are trademarks of Williamson Publishing.